DO YO

Out of luck with the ladies? Or simply … d laugh? In either case we recommend the unique volume you now hold in your hands. Within these pages you can learn how to operate The Ugly Bardot Theory, utilise The Mohawk Indian Ploy, run The Blitzkreig Technique and even turn The Noddy Formula to your advantage. These and other specialised techniques in the art of seduction are the pearls of a lifetime's dalliance, now generously strewn before the likes of you – use them wisely!

Richard Nichols is currently the editor of Custom Car *magazine and consultant editor of* Breaker. *He was actively involved in the campaign for the legalisation of CB radio and has written two books on the subject CB RADIO – A HANDBOOK and THE COMPLETE CB RADIO which is still the most comprehensive and up-to-date work available. Together with Julian Basten he is also responsible for CUSTOM CARS IN GREAT BRITAIN. He has frequently been seen on television, heard on the radio and is not to be trusted with anyone's sister.*

Also by Richard Nichols in *Star*:

CB RADIO HANDBOOK
THE COMPLETE CB RADIO
CUSTOM CARS IN GREAT BRITAIN (with Julian Basten)

DO YOU COME HERE OFTEN?

Richard Nichols

Star

A STAR BOOK
Published by
the Paperback Division of
W.H. ALLEN & CO. Ltd

A Star Book
Published in 1982
by the Paperback Division of
W.H. Allen & Co. Ltd
A Howard and Wyndham Company
44 Hill Street, London W1X 8LB

Phototypeset by Tradespools Ltd, Frome, Somerset
Printed in Great Britain by Cox & Wyman Ltd, Reading

ISBN 0 352 31173 8

Girls by Helen Ferguson
Pictures by David Leigh

Contents

ACKNOWLEDGEMENTS

During the compilation of this book it became necessary to draw on a number of personal experiences. Not all of them were especially lurid, but common sense, plus a goodly helping of cowardice, has prompted some changes. In particular you should know that the names have been changed to protect the innocent (and the not-so-innocent). In the main these people will know who they are anyway. If certain teachings of the Black Arts are to be believed then this book contains minute fragments of their souls. I would like to believe that this is true, and sincerely hope they esteem it the compliment which it is intended to be, since I remember them all with fondness, especially Barbara, Barbara, Chris, Debbie, Eileen, Evelyn, Gracie, Jan, Jan, Jane, Jo, Judy, Liz, Liz, Lynn, Mandi, Ray, Sue and Sue. Also a stunning lady I met in Captain America's in Norwich one night, whose name eludes me for the moment. And then there was . . .

Introduction

Mother of the Fair Delight
Thou handmaid perfect in God's sight
Dante Gabriel Rosetti, *Ave*

Everybody, and that includes you and I, likes to feel important at least occasionally. Very often those occasions are connected with a person's work; people like to preserve the mystique attached to their jobs, presumably in order to fend off impending redundancy. But most of us try to make our work seem difficult, with the result that there are a great many tasks which the unschooled will not take on for fear of producing an almighty cock-up. Bricklaying perhaps, or plastering, plumbing, electricianing, car-mechanicing – that order of activity. The interesting thing is that a great number of these activities are far easier than you think they are and can be performed by almost anyone providing they know what to do. The great upsurge in DIY over the past few years serves as an indication of this.

The great difficulty has previously been that innocent-sounding phrase 'providing they know what to do'. You can't guess how to wire in a ring main, or shim up the back axle of your Ford Cortina in order to compensate for wear. Either someone shows you how to do it or you glean the information from somewhere in written form. And this is where the erstwhile exponents of the previously mystical arts of bricklaying, plastering, etc, have been jolly lucky. Instead of going out of business in a dreadful slump following the huge increase in DIY some of them have managed to make even more loot by producing in written form a compilation containing all the tricks of the trade. You know the sort of thing – 'Drains Made Easy', '101 Ways to Load Your Hod', or 'Know Your Pinions', by Arthur Toolkit. That sort of thing.

In almost all of these cases the trick is to provide the unfortunate pupil with an abundance of enthusiasm coupled with just sufficient information to make the aforesaid giant cock-up without providing the knowledge needed for him to extricate himself from the resulting mess. At which point enter the bricklayers and plasterers, etc, who rush in, save the day and also make an entirely satisfactory living just as they did before.

Unless you are standing in a bookshop, reading this in your lunch break, you will already have parted with the lolly and know you've been had. Very sorry indeed. The trouble is that there is no infallible recipe for seducing beautiful women the way there are definite ways of fixing burst pipes or overheating cars.

If you are an ugly spotty individual with buck teeth then no amount of instruction in the art of conversation will transform you into a golden-haired Adonis or clear up your spots. In fact if I could invent a cure for spots I'd almost certainly make more money than I ever could writing books like this.

I can only tell you one thing. Women, whatever they would like you to believe, are immensely complicated individuals. You are, and always will be, on your own when dealing with them. After you've been married to a woman for ten years or more she will still surprise you. She'll surprise herself at the same time, but for God's sake don't expect her to admit it. All you can do is recognise women for what they are – the most beautiful of nature's creatures and the deepest of the world's mysteries, and treat them accordingly. In doing so you will never understand them, but at least you'll be in a position to enjoy them. And that's really the only rule which exists on the subject – enjoy yourself. No matter how much or how little time you spend in the company of one woman make sure you enjoy it, otherwise you'll be missing out on life's greatest pleasure, and so will the women you come into contact with, and that is surely the greatest crime you can commit.

Someone once said that beautiful women are like good wine – they improve with age and should be laid to be enjoyed. I can't, in all conscience, disagree, but I feel honour bound to point out that good wine is not something to be rushed; rather you should linger over it, savouring first its appearance, then its bouquet and then its flavour. Finally, to extract the maximum, you should allow the memory of it to haunt you forever. Only in this way can you do it justice, and be worthy of its drinking. This then, should be your real task; to be worthy of the drinking . . .

The Psychology of the Pick Up

The golden rule is that there is no golden rule
George Bernard Shaw, *Maxims for Revolutionaries*

Her name was Karen. She was only a small girl, as judged by the leggy blonde index, but for oomph and a sort of frenetic, bustling sex appeal she registered about 15 on a scale of 1–10 and about 35 on the Richter scale. At the tender age of 16 I thought she was probably the most beautiful woman in the world, possibly in the history of the world. Working behind the counter of Macdonald's (had any such thing existed at the time) she could certainly have lunched a thousand chips with little or no bother whatever.

As it was, in the South London of the late sixties, she was denied that opportunity. Even so, for someone who had given up short trousers and train spotting as recently as I, she left Helen, Cleopatra, Mata Hari and the rest of the sirens for dead. And the talent in the local Top Rank Suite, well, that lot never even got onto the card as also-rans.

I began to suspect that I might be in love. Having enjoyed no previous experience of the phenomenon it was kind of hard to tell. Being afflicted by such a condition at least explained the pounding of blood and the strange tingling sensation in certain parts of the body rather more satisfactorily than tight jeans and one of those hard leather racing saddles on the Claud Butler 10-speed.

In any case there seemed little chance that these latter two options could also account for the peculiar way in which my tongue, over which I had up till then exercised full and complete control, developed a decision-making process of its own, and knotted itself round my teeth every time Karen got within ten feet of me.

Until this moment arrived I feel it only fair to say that my immediate family and closest circle of friends would probably not have listed reticence as my most pronounced characteristic; rather the reverse was true. Consequently the strange bashfulness which affected me now was something of a novelty. As it turned out it was a novelty I could have well lived without.

At this point you should also be aware that Fate, or Lady Luck, or chemistry or whatever was actually on my side. All too often it is our lot to become madly infatuated with some extra-terrestrial goddess who remains sublimely unaware of our existence, despite the very best endeavours to reverse such a distressing situation. In this instance it was not so; Karen semed to be afflicted in the same way as I. But I have to confess at once that, at this inexperienced and untutored stage of life, I failed to observe this signally important fact for ages. Months, in fact. When this intelligence finally communicated itself to me it struck rather like one of those blinding white thunderbolts which decimate understains in detergent commercials on the telly: wham!

Were this tale one of the more tacky offerings from Hollywood or the pen of some drippy romantic novelist the time would now be right for our hero (or in this case, me) to exit stage left into the sunshine, probably in slow motion and soft-focus, hand in hand with the girl of my dreams (if such a term may be suitably applied to my somewhat lurid nocturnal imaginings). Life, as we all know, is unfortunately not like that. I wanted Karen. She, I had good reason to believe, wanted me. But 'Reason to believe', as every good copper knows, does not constitute a proven verdict.

Education, together with the general process of growing up, however slowly, had taught me how to acquire the things I needed. It taught me to work, and thus get money, how to go into a shop and get sweeties (or latterly, cigarettes) and even how to enter a pub and consume alcohol, despite the fact that I was only 16. It had not, lamentably, instructed me in the art of acquiring women.

Thus it was that, despite Karen's substantial and determined efforts to provoke me into some form of action, our youthful liaison remained unconsummated apart from a brief and heady encounter at a party which served only to confuse. Also, it frightened me to death while fortunately not quite managing to scare the pants off her.

Every cloud, we are led to believe, has a silver lining of some sort, especially if you've invested your money in clouds. Or in other words, there is something to be gained from every experience. What I gained from this particular experience was curiosity and the urge to do what my tutors had been exhorting me to do for years; try harder, and do better next time. Girls, however, were still unfamiliar territory to an ex-Boy Scout, even with 10 merit badges and the shiniest woggle in the business, and it was abundantly clear that a deeper insight was urgently needed. And the only way to gain insight on any topic is to become familiar with it. Intimate, if at all possible. And in order to achieve all this it is necessary to go where there are many girls, so without very much more ado I proceeded in the necessary direction to further my education on this most fascinating of topics.

Looking back on the events of those few months is now a decidedly painful operation. There is no doubt that the lady in question was intelligent, attractive, charming and loads more besides, so we can hardly blame her. But there's no doubt that a perfect opportunity to spend some time in the company of one so lovely was not so much missed as ignored. Rest assured that I have tried kicking myself furiously on a number of occasions; it's an improvement on sackcloth and ashes, but hardly a rewarding or fruitful experience. Banging your head against a wall is a marginal improvement and has the added advantage of affording a pleasant relief when you stop. Neither of these activities has in any way managed to compensate for the loss of this extremely desirable young lady, though, and it is at once clear that sterner stuff is called for.

The lesson is remarkably obvious, luckily, and remarkably simple also; picking up girls is definitely a two-way thing. You will seldom succeed in picking up a girl who does not wish to be picked up. Conversely it is very unlikely that you will fail to pick up a girl who wants to be picked up unless you are extremely stupid. I should know . . .

But the most important thing which emerges from this is the illuminating information that women actually want to be picked up just as much as you want to pick them up. It's obvious really. Both sexes are driven by the same urge which in its unrefined form is procreation of the species, although it may be expressed or presented in a variety of different guises depending upon circumstances, requirement and personality. There are very few ways in which women may successfully accomodate this urge other than through men; those very same men who are busy trying to achieve an exactly similar result. Whether this astonishingly complementary arrangement was all part of some divine plan is less than clear. Fortunately it is also less than relevant. It is for us to only accept that it is all a part of nature, under whose compass the process whereby two independent creatures mutually satisfy their individual needs is a repetitive theme which may be reasonably correctly described as symbiosis; quite the most polite description you're ever likely to hear.

Tradition would always have us believe that women are shy retiring creatures who prefer to hide their light under a bushel or some such, do not undress completely even for doctors and who make love only rarely, only in the bedroom and only with the lights out. While undergoing the latter process they adopt a rather fixed smile and entertain thoughts of a highly patriotic nature or mentally debate the constituents of tomorrow's cake mix. When forced to deal with the world at large they are quiet, reserved, almost withdrawn, do not hold strong or contradictory opinions, never speak loudly in restaurants or theatres and always retire to the powder room if they wish to blow their noses.

Which, incidentally, is something they almost never do. They are immune to the coarser side-effects of life, especially the ravages of strong drink and highly-spiced foods and their one desire is to remain virginal until marriage, following which they will be happiest if confined to the bedroom and the kitchen. But even in tradition there are a (very) few women who are not actually like that, and these must be regarded with grave suspicion, falling as they do into a category of medium repute at least, if not actually being hookers.

As an interesting parenthetical aside you may wish to know that a Mr Hooker actually existed. He was a General during the American Civil War, and his predilection for ladies of the night was so pronounced, his capacity so great, that the entire profession has taken its name from him, which is an inspiring accolade we would all do well to remember. And you thought the Americans had only given the world Pepsi and the Jeep . . .

Back to tradition. Which topic, highly esteemed by those who don't have any, has been taking something of a battering in recent times. This battering seems to have commenced in the 'swinging sixties' and continues up to the present day. In so far as all this relates to our chosen topic we may immediately climb straight up the nostrils of every feminist in the land and observe that the primary reason for all this appears to have been a miniature device with rather magical properties. Not the micro-chip at all, but the contraceptive pill.

As we have doubtless discovered already women are possessed of desires almost identical to those of men, and there is no reason to suppose that this is a recent development. Far more likely is that it has always been the case, but the danger of pregnancy and its lifelong consequences have always acted as a deterrent. It has always been the woman who has suffered the stigma of unmarried parenthood and always been the woman who has been forced to shoulder the resultant burden. The advent of the pill has all but eliminated the risks and obviated the need for women to repress their natural instincts. This has left them free to act as they choose, which can only be a Good Thing, although it is taking Society at large rather longer to come to terms with this than many individual women.

What it means to you is not that the world is full of a larger number of women who are free and easy than was previously the case, but simply that all of them have as much freedom of action as you do, which was never the case before. Consequently the most difficult part of picking up women is no longer an obstacle. You need not regard all women as a challenge to your ability with the smooth chat, nor as an exercise in duplicity, ever again. Accept, then, that women think much as you do.

The only problems which remain before you are now of your own making, and we shall deal with many of them individually and in greater depth. For the moment we'll remain with generalities.

Out shopping one Saturday morning, I could hardly fail to notice a young-ish couple, hand-in-hand, window gazing outside a jewellers' shop. As chance would have it she was looking at substantially-priced rings containing the sort of diamond which would make a suitable foundation stone for a prestigious and exceptionally tall building. He on the other hand was far more concerned with the type of electronic timing device which reveals the state of the tide in Honolulu as well as measuring the duration of a flea's sneeze to seven decimal places. A reasonably revealing insight into human nature, but not the thing which impinged upon the consciousness of the casual observer. What I, and most others in the area, noticed primarily was the dimensions of the happy couple. Stout is not the word for it. Fat is the only thing which will suffice. They were, in fact, clearly constructed by the same firm responsible for Falstaff and probably victims of the same sort of gluttony which left Winnie-the-Pooh corking up Rabbit's front door for a week.

'There is,' observed my companion, 'someone for everyone.' Thing of it is, she was dead right. There is. But now comes the $64,000 question; how do you know which one is yours? Let's assume that there are 60 million people in the country. Let's further assume that half of them are women.

Now let's asume that this 30 million is evenly divided so that there are equal numbers of women of every age between one and 65. Let us now decide that we are interested only in those between, say, 16 and 36. That means that there are nine million women out there. If only one of them was yours you'd be in really big trouble, wouldn't you? You wouldn't know whether to start in Birmingham or Widdybank Fell. Despite the rather discouraging sound of all this things are not all that bad, for nature has intervened on your behalf. You will have observed for yourself that you are passingly attracted to more than one woman. More than one a week, even. Possibly more than one a day, even more than one every hour. In extreme cases you may even be attracted to them in bunches of 10 and over. This does not necessarily indicate that you are some kind of sex-crazed fiend (although you may be one of the lucky few) but rather that you are less than minutely selective.

Most of you will be aware of this already. There is a saying; 'Gentlemen prefer blondes'. It might be true. They may well, but they'll take what they can get. Some quirk of nature which nobody understands at all has brought about an eminently satisfactory solution to this otherwise insurmountable problem of multiple choice. It may be heredity, genetic chance or some factor of early life which comes into play here, but most people find that their selectivity is not a major limiting factor, although it will always narrow the field.

There's a lot of old toss talked about the 'perfect woman'; you know, Joan Bakewell's brain, face like Debbie Harry, body like Raquel Welch, bank balance like Christina Onassis and the instincts of Emmanuelle. Personally I'd settle for the estimable Ms Bakewell any day. You will almost certainly disagree, which illustrates the point admirably; there's no such thing as a perfect woman for all men, nor even for any man, but most men will know that the women they are attracted to tend to share a great number of characteristics with each other. Maybe it's blue-eyed blondes, dark-eyed brunettes, green-eyed redheads, ladies with, shall we say, a giant pair of equal opportunities, skinny girls, tall girls, short girls, anything. Maybe it's not even that obvious. Maybe it's a sense of humour, a high degree of intelligence, pronounced sensitivity. More than likely it will be a combination of many things.

Since physical appearance is the first thing which you will notice about any human being this obviously plays an important role, though you may not be aware of it, but if you think about it you'll find that there is probably a common thread. I find eyes of great importance; not the colour so much as the content, since they are extremely expressive and the hardest thing to falsify. Look at someone's eyes and you'll find out a great deal, and there's little that can be done to prevent it. After that, I tend to head for small slim women, the majority of whom are dark-haired, although this is not always true. I like intelligence, love a sense of humour and need sensitivity.

Out of these nine million women in the country two million are too young for me, three million too old. That leaves only four million to choose from. Half of these will be blonde, half of the remainder rather big for my taste and who knows how many of the remaining million share my particular brand of humour? Straight away your task is made easier, since you are doubtless able to apply similar precepts of your own.

It would not do for you to apply them too rigidly, though. I know that it is quite within the bounds of possibility for me to share great pleasure with tall humourless blondes of Scandinavian extraction, and you would be doing yourself (and the ladies of the world) a great disservice if you ignored large numbers of them on what is, after all, a rather arbitrary basis. But content yourself with the knowledge that there is a group of women with the right kind of appearance and style to which you are most likely to be susceptible.

Women, of course, will subconsciously be as subject to this kind of whimsical choice as you are, and it is at this point that we should be even more pleased that nature has seen fit to arrange things to maximum advantage. Because

the chances are that the type of woman you are attracted to will, on a great number of occasions, be successfully able to classify you as the type of man she is attracted to. Quite why this fortunate coincidence should be true remains something of a mystery, although it may not be the burning question of the hour, nor even be as important as the identity of the gunman who shot JR. But whether it be happy accident or something more sinister bears little relevance to the effect.

One explanation for it may rest in the 'magical chemistry' bit to which so many pithy romantic novelists subscribe. This is the sort of effect which probably accounts for the 'Romeo and Juliet Syndrome', the 'Cathy and Heathcliff Law' and similar instances of what is endearingly termed love at first sight. You know the score; two pairs of eyes meet across a crowded room, a banal exchange of pleasantries takes place and in the ensuing coupling (which takes place within the mandatory maximum of thirty seconds after the first meeting) the only thing which is satisfied is the censor's red pen.

However there may be more to all this than, ahem, meets the eye. Let us be in no doubt that despite the trappings of civilisation, the natty gents' tailoring, the Balmain gowns and the raising of little fingers while supping daintily at the breakfast cornflakes, we are but animals after all. As such we are as subject to natural laws as a pair of alleycats when it comes to encounters with the opposite sex, romantic or simply frantic.

To begin with there is no doubt whatever that human beings produce natural body musks in exactly the same way as dogs and cats, although we may not spend our lives urinating on lamposts and rubbing our glands all over each other. These scents will pass messages on to those around us, on all sorts of different subjects. In particular they will inform members of both sexes in sufficiently close proximity when we are ill, aggressive, enraged or, more to the point, aroused.

Upon the receipt of this last piece of intelligence a woman will respond. She will *know* that you are, shall we say, interested. There is no question about this. Do not for a moment continue in the erroneous belief that she is oblivious to your feelings, because she isn't. Although this may save you the need for weedy remarks in the 'cor, I don't half fancy you' vein there is no call to think that the hunt is over and done with and that all that remains is for you to carry off your prize in suitably macho fashion. This is not true. The lady may well be aware of your condition. She may not, however, reciprocate. If she does it will be your job to determine that she has and then take further steps along the path to Nirvana, or Neasden, or wherever it is you live.

You will determine the required information initially by the same means which she exercised on you. You won't be aware of a sudden gush of highly stimulating odour beneath your nostrils, so don't waste your time sniffing like a demented bloodhound. Rather you will be subconsciously aware that you are doing something right and will thus be encouraged to continue. You may wish to believe that she is fascinated by your colourful description of how you sailed single-handed down the Orinoco, pursued by bloodthirsty cannibals, and armed with nothing more than a pencil-sharpener and the AA Guide to Caravan Sites in Europe. You may think it's the disgustingly expensive aftershave you're wearing. You may be right, but the chances are you're wrong. But it doesn't matter, because what will happen now is that, emboldened by whatever fallacious belief you are cherishing at this moment, you will lean in closer in order to maximise result, thus giving the lady a more concentrated blast of your personal musks and intensifying their action upon her subconscious.

Even more important, your adrenalin will be surging through your body, although it may be difficult to distinguish this effect from the startlingly similar feeling induced by the bottle and a half of brandy you have downed in the past five minutes. No matter. The adrenalin will perform the required tasks quite unaided by any human agency, which is just as well, because with that lot inside you your condition could hardly be summarised as human.

What will happen now is that the pupils of your eyes will dilate quite noticeably and Madam will not fail to spot this salient occurrence. With average luck she will decline to accept this as evidence of advanced alcohol poisoning and will interpret it in the traditional fashion, taking it to mean that you are even more aroused than you were when you were only smelly. Before you dismiss this as rubbish, listen to this.

Some while ago there was a TV programme fronted by someone clever and jovial, which means it was probably James Burke. One item was of overwhelming interest to us at this point. James invited a male volunteer to step forward from the audience, and one duly did so, since there is never any shortage of clowns who are willing to be humiliated in the interest of the great God of the goggle-box. The victim, for that is really the only description which may be properly applied to such unfortunates, was made to stand with his back to the stage. 'In a moment,' crowed the presenter, 'two attractive young girls will walk onto the stage behind you. When I give the word – wait for it – I want you to slowly turn round in a complete circle until you are facing the audience again, and then I will ask you a question. Because I am a TV star and therefore ten times smarter than you I already know what your answer will be and I have taken the precaution of writing it on a piece of paper which is contained within this sealed envelope I am holding.' While the TV presenter had been chatting two stunningly attractive ladies had materialised on stage behind the victim. They were lovely. So lovely that it was hard to tell which was the more attractive of the two. This dilemma was further complicated by the fact that the two girls were identical blonde twins.

The victim performed a clumsy pirouette. 'Now then,' quizzed The Personality, 'which of those two did you find most attracted you as a man?' The audience laughed on cue, probably without the prompt boards. 'The one on the left,' answered the victim. He was, not surprisingly, allowed to open the envelope himself to discover that The Personality had indeed predicted his answer correctly. 'Do you know why?' queried our genial host. Of course the victim, who was probably sweating on account of having a large and ferocious wife lurking in the audience, rolling-pin akimbo, stammered a bit and failed to come up with a suitable reply. Which was just as well for The Personality, whose thunder would have been well and truly half-inched had the victim been aware of the backstage machinations immediately prior to the show.

What had happened was quite simple. Very simple, in fact. The twin on the left had been doctored. Somebody had administered a small quantity of eye-drops which had caused the pupils of her eyes to temporarily dilate to incredible proportions. Human beings recognise this as a sign of great sexual interest and arousal, and the poor victim had been unable to prevent his subconscious from noticing and responding. Our host assured us that he could repeat this phenomenon endlessly and without fail, which is most interesting and serves to confirm what we have said.

In particular a marked display of interest on the part of one person will always produce an automatic result in a member of the opposite sex, even where no previous inclination existed. Further you should now know that a woman's eyes will give you more clues as to your progress than almost anything she says. Slinky blondes who whisper things like 'Hello, big boy, is that a gun in your pocket or are you just pleased to see me?' while smelling neutral and retaining pinpricks where other girls have eyes are definitely not inviting you to participate in a frenzied orgy, although they may do so later once your irresistible charm has laid low their defences.

This should not be taken as an instruction to start squirting all kinds of obnoxious and toxic substances into your eyes in an effort to make it into the lounge lizard top ten; nature will do the necessary on your behalf in any event.

But you may wish to consider the prospect of a new scent for men which has recently made its way onto the market. Scientists believe they have isolated the musks which indicate arousal and therefore attract women. Although technology has not yet reached the point at which they can offer it as a freeze-dried dietary adjunct heavily buffered in monosodium glutamate and available in the Co-op in family-size packs, it has been crammed into an aerosol spray and can be purchased in a selection of specialist emporiums at a suitably horrendous price. Much experimentation, particularly by various media outlets, has so far failed to produce conclusive endorsement for this product on an overall basis, but it is already clear that it is surprisingly efficacious in some cases. This would appear to be a reflection of the principle whereby some expensive after-shaves smell delectable on some men but are more than slightly reminiscent of diesel oil on others. It's apparently all down to body chemistry. Nonetheless it provides clear scientific evidence that natural scents are vitally important in this sort of sexual skirmishing, especially in its early stages.

So. What with social emancipation, the pill, procreation being the strongest instinct after self-preservation, a plethora of rat-like odours and soulful saucerlike eyes brimming with empathy, sensitivity and fascination (not to mention unbridled lust), it would seem that you can hardly miss. You, however, are hardly that gullible, even though you may continue to purchase vast amounts of a soap powder you neither need nor like simply because it's being advertised on the telly by a triffic-looking blonde with an eyeful of chemicals. You are well aware that it is still not that easy to gain intimate access to the person and personality of vast numbers of women. But you are at least in a position to shorten the odds.

Robert the Bruce, aside from being an individual of a Scottish disposition, and demonstrating a pronounced, if slightly unusual, fondness for spiders, has a great deal to answer for at this point. 'If at first you don't succeed . . .' etc, may be an inspiring example. However it does not benefit you greatly to take this to extremes. WC Fields, who quite sensibly took his hatred of small children and fondness for alcohol to the point at which they ceased to be extreme and became legendary, learnt from the spider rather more than did Robert the Bruce. 'If at first you don't succeed,' said WC, 'try, try again. Then quit. There's no point making a fool of yourself.' This is a remarkably entertaining piece of sagacity which you would do well to consider.

We have spoken, up to now, of generalities, which is all as it should be, and shall speak a great deal more of them within a very short space of time. Specifics, tedious though they may be, are not something we can afford to ignore.

Here you are, then, out and about in the normal run of events, and suddenly confronted with an attractive young lady. Whether or not she fits into the stereotype identikit picture of the sort of woman you mostly find stimulating is a matter of insignificance. What's more important is simply that you find her attractive. Armed with the certain knowledge that she cannot fail to become aware of your interest, you steam in straight off, emanating musks like a supercharged skunk and with your eyes so wide open they're in imminent danger of falling into your soup. Or worse still, her soup. While eyeballs are considered to be a great delicacy in certain far-flung corners of Arabia they are not generally greeted with the same sort of enthusiasm in Chelsea.

Madam retains her reserve; unmoved, she is presenting a creditable impersonation of an unknown glacier somewhere in the Antarctic. All is not as well as it should be, and someone is doing something wrong. You won't need to sniff heavily or glare at her eyes to confirm this, because your subconscious will have informed you already, and you know that you're dying on your feet, taking more flak than a humourless comedian in a Northern Working Man's Club. The trouble is that you will not have been able to detect all this until you got in close. It is at this juncture that you should heed the advice of WC and knock it on the head at once. Excuse yourself, in any one of a variety of ways which seem appropriate (expressions like 'pony', or oblique references to a girl's best friend should be avoided at all costs) and naff off damn quick. Retire to the nearest bar and, while replenishing your ego, analyse what has taken place.

You have clearly made an unwelcome attempt to enter forbidden territory. The truth is that a great number of women are simply unavailable, to you or anyone else. It's possible that they are only unavailable to you, and failures of this nature are not only unavoidable they are to be expected. If such events become a regular feature of your life while the women who reject you quite happily make friends with other men – take stock of yourself. Large numbers of women object to men who are dirty, unshaven, have hair growing from their ears or who have runny noses; ladies like this tend also to be unimpressed by offensive odours. Even today a lot of women abhor language which you may choose to believe is simply earthy or colourful and which they perceive as vulgar and insulting. All of these things can be corrected. Correct them. If you are possessed of a demeanour and appearance which would make Quasimodo attractive by comparison you're in real trouble, and may well find that there is little hope for you and your dreams of sexual fulfilment; perhaps you should consider religion. The power of prayer is unlikely to effect any sort of metamorphosis and you are unlikely to wake up one morning looking like Robert Redford; however I understand that a large number of monastic orders, especially the silent ones, are quite sympathetic to this sort of thing.

If none of the foregoing applies then you must do three things. One: breathe a deep sigh of relief. Two: have another drink. Three: decide what went wrong.

We know that women are not unlike you in outlook and ultimate goal, but it is unreasonable to expect all of them to fall at your feet swooning with desire. There will be failures, and you must accept these as philosophically as you can. After all, not even Steve Davis pots everything he aims at. Setbacks are a natural part of the grand design, so don't get upset.

But what you can do is to make sure that you suffer the minimum number of them; the maxim here is do not waste your time on something which is doomed to failure from the outset.

For a kick-off, some women are married or engaged.

While modern enlightenment has meant that this need not mean you should automatically write such ladies off your shopping list it is a fair pointer to the likely outcome, and while you're playing percentages that's what counts. Married or engaged women tend to take pleasure in announcing the fact via the medium of gold rings or housebricks masquerading as diamonds. These tend to be worn on the third finger, left hand. This is particularly convenient since you will be able to spot such a device from a considerable distance and thus spare two people a great deal of unnecessary embarrassment.

Rings of this type need not be interpreted as a 'trespassers will have their heart and liver torn out by my six-foot 220 lb rugby-playing husband, who just happens to be a sergeant in the SAS' sign, but they should be taken into consideration.

The possibility also exists that married ladies with 2.3 children and a husband who drives the company Cortina home to a semi in Cheam at 5.30 every night do not wear a wedding ring. In this case you could still encounter a brick wall.

There are still several avenues of information-gathering open to you. Eyes are important here as well. Look at the lady again and see what she looks at; it may be possible that she is flirting quite shamelessly with you over a long distance just by the use of eye contact. In our crowded world people – men and women – tend to avoid over-long eye contact with strangers, thus signalling disinterest and a desire to avoid conflict. If she holds your gaze too long or too boldly . . . Likewise they avoid physical contact, except when trying to get to the bar before you or steal your place at the checkout queue in Tesco. The way they sit or stand is a sign as well. Those who wish to remain anonymous and unapproachable will draw their limbs in, folding up their body in a way that tends to make it unobtrusive. People who get on well together tend to adopt each other's positioning and mannerism. They stand, sit or lie in similar positions. If someone on the tube or in a pub starts what appears to be a dance routine – make sure it's a woman.

Women make the same kind of signals to men; the languid crossing of a pair of well-turned and silk-clad ankles is the oldest cinema cliché in the book, but it has a solid foundation in reality and constitutes a definite invitation, especially when combined with a wide-eyed stare.

A word of warning. Take your surroundings into account and, if need be, beware of hookers.

This kind of body-talk is not only commonplace but also long-established. Its roots are buried well into the past. It's a subliminal method of communication which the human race has been practising for much longer than other means, including language. It is still one of the primary means of communications among animals, as anyone who watches BBC2 is doubtless well aware. Since this is true it is unlikely that you can be taught anything on the subject which you did not already know, and the best thing you can do is remember that it exists and then use it to influence your actions. In other words you will do extremely well to follow what we may rightly call your instincts.

So if you feel that a particular woman doesn't want to have anything to do with you, even before you've spoken to her, you're probably right, whatever your reasoning and your opinion of your masculine charm may indicate. If your common sense tells you that a certain woman couldn't possibly harbour the faintest desire even to share a seat on the bus with you but your instincts are screaming the opposite – press on.

None of this provides a fixed ruling for any given situation. But you should be aware of it all the same, and use the information to maximum advantage always, both to save foul-ups and embarrassment on all sides as well as to enjoy the many pleasures life lays in your path.

They are all generalities still, however useful they may be. All they can do is encourage you to trust your instincts and use them to eliminate the impossible and concentrate on the probable unless you are the sort of person who really likes a challenge and would be quite at home attempting to scale the North face of the Eiger wearing only Bermuda shorts and with one hand tied to the tail of a ferocious man-eating lion.

Meanwhile the rest of us will turn up the central heating, top up our glasses and settle back in a comfy chair to assess the situation so far. We know the women are out there, and we know that they are as anxious to meet us as we are to meet them. We even know roughly how to pick out the disinterested types in a crowd, and from a reasonably safe distance. We can also gauge with some accuracy the degree of success or failure we are attaining once we are close enough to read the signs. But first it is necessary to get close enough.

The Body in Question – Yours

Free your armpits from the ram and the goat
Ovid, *Advice to Suitors*

Here we are then, all set to go out into the big wide world and meet lots of women. All of whom, it need not be pointed out, will necessarily fall madly in love with you on the spot and thus be desperately anxious for you to transport them at once, if not sooner, to your fairy-tale castle in Spain or Neasden, or wherever, where you may spend the rest of your life transporting them even further to the heights of ecstasy. But therein lies the problem; once you've got them where they want you, what are you going to do about it? And before that how indeed are you going to get them where they want you?

Ages ago, during the days of the *pax Romana*, they used to say that being made Emperor was easy. It was keeping the title (and, incidentally, your head) which was the hard part. In our case, or rather yours, the situation is reversed – provided always that you apply a modicum of good sense, and treat women like human beings. We'll get to that bit later. Much later. Meanwhile we're more interested in the first part of the exercise; getting them.

Now we come to the first hurdle. While writing something of this nature it is hard to avoid speaking of women in a rather dispersonal fashion, and regarding them as the quarry, in much the same way as landed gentry tend to look on Charles James, or The Varmint (foxes, to you, gonzo). This however is not in your best interests while you are at the sharp end. Doubtless you've already read countless men's magazines, in particular all the rather breathless bits of fiction and in some cases the letters page, and noticed the bits where women have these fantasies about being sex objects, and being pursued by giant macho-men who treat them like dirt, constantly ignore them, beat them and generally drag them around by the hair, figuratively if not literally. However, beware – most of the fiction and a great deal of the letters are penned by hands which are unmistakeably male, which casts a somewhat biased shadow over the entire proceedings.

Don't be entirely put off, though. There is little doubt that at some time, or times, in their lives, most women are partial to what may be colloquially described as 'a bit of rough'. Likewise a great number of women entertain fantasies during which they indubitably do enjoy being treated as objects by suitably well-built and handsome males. This process, however, serves only to confuse the situation rather than simplify it.

For a start you will, unless you are clairvoyant or have crystal balls, come up against the problem of timing. Yes, women sometimes fancy a bit of rough. But when is sometimes? You won't be able to tell by looking, that's for sure. And if you have to stop and ask you will already have ruled yourself out as a prize wally. And then even if you do, by some miracle of timing, happen to bruise along at exactly the correct moment, you could still run into problems.

To begin with, all these fantasies of macho-men are just that: fantasies. Practically none of the women who enjoy such idle daydreams will ever relish the prospect of them coming to fruition. All these breathless ladies who write lascivious letters to *Mayfair* and similar, all about being the centrepiece in a Hell's Angels gang-bang, would be horrified if the translation into reality ever took place. Best thing is to leave dreams where they belong – in the head. Encourage them within the context of an already-extant relationship, sure, but that's another chapter altogether, and doesn't appear for several pages yet. First, *cherchez la femme*.

As a final cautionary note, take advice on this. In nearly all fantasies of this nature you will find out of an imaginary gang of 50 greasy, smelly motorcyclists, 10 resemble Robert Redford in a more than passing fashion, 10 are not totally removed from Bogart during his *Casablanca* period, another 10 are Mick Jagger without the make-up and yet another 10 will have a faint resemblance to Reginald Bosanquet or Robert Dougall. The final 10 will almost certainly look rather like John Hurt in his role as The Elephant Man, for whom nearly every woman in the world nurtured a sizeable amount of maternal sympathy. However the permutations run you may rest assured that none of the assembled company will look even faintly like Norman Arthur Putey, Chartered Accountant, of Laburnum Crescent. Or you. Or me, come to that.

It will only ever be by fortunate accident that you turn up next to a woman who is nursing a particular fantasy into which you just happen to fit like the missing bit of a 500-piece jigsaw puzzle. When that does happen – make the most of it. But don't spent the rest of your life mooching about waiting for the moment. There are far more concrete and more readily-realisable opportunities available to you. The two questions which must be answered now are whether or not you are ready for them and then whether or not you're worthy of them.

The answer to both is probably not. I'm not, and I'm writing the book. Let's go back to the beginning, which is where all the best things should start, despite what Harold Robbins might say on the subject. Right then. Are you ready? You might think so, which is all very well. But if by some miracle you should find that later this evening all your dreams on the subject are realised, and a delectable lady is wrapped in your arms, you may discover that come the stroke of midnight she will vanish. In all probability she won't turn back into a pumpkin, but then she probably won't leave you with a conveniently-sized glass slipper through which you can trace her either. Was it something you said? Or something you did? Or, far more likely, was it something you didn't say or didn't do? Let's leave sayings for a while, and concentrate on doings.

I can remember, when I was a kid, that my mother used to make me take a bath regularly. I can also recall hating the prospect, which led to the ridiculous situation in which I would lock myself in the bathroom, run a tub full of hot water and then sit on the bathstool, reading a good book while occasionally stirring the water with one foot, thus making highly realistic washing noises. This ploy satisfied all parties concerned for a number of years, and also enabled me to read a number of fine books which I might otherwise have missed out of my curriculum entirely.

While such an arrangement may well be eminently satisfactory for small boys of tender years, also for the publishers of *Biggles*, it has little to commend itself to grown-up boys who have recently given up train-spotting in favour of the local disco.

One thing I can promise you. While you are gently wafting the lady of your choice around the dance floor in lazy circles and idly dreaming of the great things you will do together she is remembering all the practical advice her mother gave her, however liberated she may be or wish to appear as being. Among such advice will be vast tracts on the subject of personal hygiene. For entirely plausible reasons beyond my control women are obliged to pay greater attention to this sort of thing on a functionally biological level than men. Following hard on the heels of this they are bombarded with advertising messages which exhort them to take all this to a more esoteric level, in consequence of which they are liable to splash themselves liberally with various perfumed substances which will guarantee that Paul Newman will ask them out at least twice a week. Before that come the preparatory confections which deep-clean their skin, give them healthy pores, prevent wrinkles, feed and nourish their natural hormones and give them that fresh-all-over glow which they may later successfully submerge beneath several layers of proprietary chemicals which do the same only more so.

Women, in case you've missed the point, tend to be clean. At the very least. Most of them regard this state as being a compliment to Paul Newman and other males who they expect to take an interest in them. As a result of this they also expect that their men should at least repay the compliment. Now though a hard-working husband or boyfriend, fresh from the garage or garden on a Sunday afternoon, may present an endearing sight in old roll-neck, jeans and wellies, covered variously in manure, mud, prunings from the rose-bushes and several ancient substances which, despite a pronounced and horrific odour, remain unidentified, this is not on for the likes of you.

The appearance and smell of hard work, a collection of dead insects from the garage floor in the hair, plus an assortment of black sticky things between the teeth is all very well in its place. The disco isn't it. So while you are spinning round to the latest in the disco-groper's top ten, remember that her mind is elsewhere. If you forgot to wash behind your ears she will spot it before you cross the dance floor to make with that wonderfully successful chat of yours. If you've still got the contents of a Morris Minor sump up your nose remember it'll be that she's looking at with disgust when you think she's gazing adoringly into your eyes. And if it doesn't stop her dancing with you it'll sure as hell make her run for the bus alone when they start playing *The Last Waltz*.

So. Start at the beginning. Before you go anywhere near a woman upon whose person you entertain desires, or anywhere near a place in which women who may inspire such desires are wont to congregate – make sure that you have ruthlessly eradicated all traces of your day's adventures from your person.

And think on this. Most of the time the women you meet and with whom you wish to spend a little of your oh-so-precious time will be chance encounters; in the office, the library, the pub at lunchtime, whatever. At those unexpected moments would it not be truly dreadful if you bore the aspect and aroma of a particularly foul by-product of some noxious organic process normally associated with the slaughter of camels or some such? Of course it would. And not only would it be truly dreadful, it would also render your chances of success roughly equivalent to the prospect of meeting Debbie Harry in the local Wimpy bar.

The golden rule, therefore, is be prepared. You don't have to wear the stubbies (Strine for shorts) or the silly hat, or even a woggle. Just be ready. You can buy posters in a lot of shops which bear the legend 'Tomorrow is the first day of the rest of your life'. It could also be the day you meet Debbie Harry in the Wimpy bar. Will you be ready for it? If the answer is no – go take a bath at once.

Now. Taking a bath can, if treated correctly, be something of a pleasure in itself, and as this is the first step along your long road to the ultimate realisation of all your physical expectations it would be a great shame (and a poor omen) if you were to embark upon the action without due regard to the niceties of the situation. Make the most of it. It has come to my attention over the years that many people regard bathing as something of an ordeal, and view the entire performance with the same kind of esteem which they would normally accord a dead ferret. This is purely because they have been going about the whole thing in the wrong fashion. There are several items which are essential to a successful bathtime. The first of these is, naturally, a bath. We must assume that you've got one of those. If you haven't then there probably isn't a woman within a hundred miles of you anyway, in which case we've all been wasting our time. I do, however, have it on good authority that some of God's creatures are not overly concerned with personal hygiene. None of them resemble women in any materially important fashion. Nor can any of them, to my knowledge, provide your breakfast scrambled eggs and coffee to the correct consistency, so it would be better if you didn't waste your time. Under such circumstances I can do little more than quote Woody Allen, who said of masturbation 'It's only sex with someone you love'. It also means never having to say you're sorry, and further allows that you don't have to look your best. In the light of this information all those without baths can clear off at once. There's a policeman looking for you anyway.

The rest of us, having assured ourselves of the existence of the tub, may safely proceed to the next step. Heat. Hot baths are great. Forget all that stuff you read in *Tom Brown's Schooldays* and similar. Hot baths are where it's at. Hot baths in cold bathrooms are prejudicial to your enjoyment. Make sure the bathroom is hot too. Fill the tub with hot water. Take off all your clothes and get in. Now get out again, you've forgotten loads of essentials.

You will need, in no special order, a musical device of some sort, like a radio, a soft towel or similar upon which to rest your head while you read the truly excellent book or magazine with which you have so thoughtfully provided yourself, cigarettes if you are so inclined, and a drink of some sort. In the sultry atmosphere of your bathroom you will find that a bottle of extremely cold white wine is a special treat. Failing that a very dry Martini – almost all gin, with a vermouth content which is only as much as is left on the rim of your glass when rubbed with the cork from the bottle – will suffice. Don't forget to shake it over ice and include a particularly succulent olive.

At this point you will find it especially beneficial if all the accessories – soap, facecloth, towel, etc – are readily to hand. Prepare this before you get into the water.

Now lie back and relax. Top up the tub with hot water from time to time. Continue to do this for as long as your drink/book/magazine lasts, or until your fingertips go all crinkly and you can no longer manipulate the controls. You will find that if you gently pull the plug prior to topping-up all the cold water which, for some immensely complicated reason is all at the bottom anyway, runs out, allowing the maintenance of the temperature level you desire as well as the ingress of further supplies of hot water without the need to summon the RNLI when you wish to emerge from the bathroom.

Before you do your Venus de Milo impression and depart from the water don't forget the reason for being there in the first place. Do remember to scrub yourself all over, especially those private places which not even certain kinds of lager can reach. Then you can leave.

Next step – wash your hair and shave. Don't do either of those while you are actually in the bath itself, however temptingly easy it may be. If you wash your hair, even before you attend to laundering the rest of your anatomy, you will fill the bath up with slimy white stuff, which after only a few moments will bear not even the slightest resemblance to those fragrant bubbles you saw in all the ads. You know what it looks like . . . Shaving will fill the entire bath with more little hairs than you could ever believe possible. When you climb out they will stick to you, and not even the most thorough towelling will remove them. Later on this evening, when you start to get warm on the dance floor, they will begin to irritate worse than an attack of mosquitoes (or something less appealing). And you, my friend, aren't going to look that enticing if you're stood on the edge of the dance floor surreptitiously scratching your naughty bits. Doesn't matter how discreet you think you're being, *everyone*, and especially her, will spot what you're up to straight away. And you may rest assured that while you may not know what they're thinking, one thing which won't be at the forefront of their minds is 'there's a bloke who shaved in the bath tonight'. 'Kay?

Next bit. Go to the mirror. Avoid singing snatches from *Tommy*. Examine your face. Make sure it's clean and you didn't miss any bits with the razor. Now look at it carefully again. See that pointed job with two holes sticking out in the middle? That's a nose, but I'm sure you knew that anyway, didn't you? Of course you did, because you use it for all sorts of things, especially those with an olfactory connection.

If someone puts a plate of food in front of you your immediate assessment of the nature of such victuals will be made on the basis of sight (which we'll deal with later) and smell. If it smells good you're anticipating that it will taste nice. If the reverse is true, then the reverse is true. Now consider this. Food isn't the only thing which your nose informs you about and, to a fair extent, colours your

judgement of. All sorts of things come under this scrutiny. Anything with a discernible odour is subject to the vagaries of its opinion, whether the idea appeals to you or not.

Women have noses too. You are one of the things which they will unconsciously examine and report on. It is obvious that your case will be greatly enhanced, if not actually advanced, should the results of this examination prove favourable. Standing as you are now, fresh from your bath, there is little doubt of your success in this matter, unless you suffer from an advanced glandular condition, in which case see a doctor, or stick to goats, who are less likely to be offended by this sort of thing.

Assuming that you're still with us, and not en route to the clinic or the nearest zoo, let us proceed. You've passed the test now, but what of later? After a hectic half-hour on a hot sweaty dance floor? All the good work you've done in the tub is liable to be precipitately undone unless you take immediate steps to prevent it. Deodorant is what you need, and now, before the rot sets in.

There are various types available to you and it really is a question of personal choice; aerosols are easy but they're bloody cold and the propellant tends to leave nasty marks on your shirts. But it's up to you. Don't be deluded into thinking that this is an unnecessary step, or that using a deodorant will turn you into a practising homosexualist overnight. It isn't, and it won't. And I promise that women will appreciate it.

It's perfectly true that scent plays a fairly large part in the interplay between men and women, especially in bed, and it's quite true that natural musks, such as are released by glands all over your body and particularly under your arms, do act as a stimulant. But in this, as in most other things with the fair sex, it's the light touch which is the winner. If you get close enough to a woman tonight for her to be able to catch your personal musk and react to it, the exercise in which you will doubtless be indulging will release enough of it to overcome any man-made perfumes you may be wearing. You don't actually want rivers of perspiration gushing all over the place.

And women respond just as much to pleasant synthetic perfumes as they do to the natural kind. At this point you may well wish to consider the possibility of using aftershave of some sort. Again this is a matter for personal opinion. It is also another touchy subject among some men who are afraid that their masculinity will suffer if they use any sort of perfume. I can absolutely promise you that using aftershave will not make your naughty bits wither and drop off, so there's no need to worry on that score. Neither will it prevent you from enjoying the company and comforts of women. There is a small possibility that a few other men may regard you as being about as straight as a nine-bob note if you smell nice, but then ask yourself: who's taking an attractive woman home tonight? It won't be the sweaty bastard in the corner who's been laughing at you all evening. Now who's a jessie?

If you do use aftershave already, or if you start today, you will at once be apprised of a very relevant factor. It's bloody expensive stuff. Under such circumstances it is in your best interests to maximise your benefits while minimising your costs. This doesn't mean you should only use it on special occasions. We've already established that you won't know when Madam Fortune, or at least somebody of her gender, is going to come knocking on your door, so use it always. But don't drown yourself in it.

To begin with, and more often if you wet-shave, you'll want to put it on your face because it'll make it feel better. After that there are places you can put it which will give the best results. And you can stop sniggering right now, because that's not what I mean. Anyway, it stings. There are some parts of your body which already produce your own scent or which exude a natural oil. These areas will hold and enhance any scent you add to them as will the heat generated by pulse points at your neck and wrists. Ask yourself why women put perfume where they do: behind their ears, on the back of their neck, inside their wrists and elbows. It's because they've been taught to be mean with precious commodities and they know how to get the best out of them. You could do a lot worse than follow their example so start tonight.

One other thing. Did you know that, for some eminently plausible reason that escapes me entirely, the nail on your index finger grows faster than all the others? Most women think this is the sort of thing men should know. It would be a great help if your fingernails were clean and neatly trimmed . . .

Now then. If you've done everything correctly you should be clean and shiny, and smelling sweeter than all the other geezers. That's the trick, you see. The world is full of other men, all trying to do a runner with the lady you fancy. All you can do is make sure you're not offensive and then try to stand out from the rest of the crowd.

You're ready to get dressed. First, recharge your drink. Now proceed to your dressing-room. This will of course be at a sensible temperature, unless you're practising those terrible Nanook of the North impressions of yours. See you in the bedroom . . .

Ah, there you are. Now, let's have a look at you.

What we're after at this point is deciding how you are going to appear in the eyes of the world. Like it or not a great many people do allow first impressions to colour, if not actually inflame their opinion of others. Even worse news for you is that the percentage of people who think in this regrettable manner contains a great number of women, particularly the ones you're interested in. Whether you like or not, therefore, you will have to take this distressing information into account, and all previous remarks on the subject of old roll-necks and camel-dung apply only more so. Even though this is true there is no point in going overboard. Doubtless you've heard Fred Wedlock's amusing little ditty on the subject of ancient and overdressed swingers and know I'm not kidding. There is little benefit in trying to be something which you transparently are not. This is an exceedingly useful rule which applies to every aspect of the subject currently in hand and also in a great many respects to the subject you are attempting to take in hand as well.

And this does not only relate to those among us who have

reached a stage in life at which sartorial choice begins to assume a more limited aspect; even sprightly and youthful types will look ridiculous if they step too far out of the area in which they rightly belong, so you can pack in sniggering up your sleeve for a start.

Therefore the best thing you can do at this stage is examine yourself as critically as possible and eliminate the obvious no-nos. For example an 18-year-old, 96 lb spotty weakling will look ridiculous togged up like a lumberjack, although current punk-like trends in clothing will suit admirably. Likewise portly, red-faced old gentlemen of 50-plus will do well to avoid dyeing their hair in a variety of startling primary colours and putting diamond studs through the side of their noses. Fashion, even for men, is doubtless a wonderful thing, but you need not follow it too slavishly. It will thus be apparent that you need to develop some form of dress sense if you are not lucky enough to possess it already. In this you will be much aided by the many publications on the market aimed specifically at men.

These magazines tend to carry, among the various other subjects on show, a substantial proportion of features on fashion and various other topics. In the main this is because it is necessary to have one general feature in order for them to avoid being labelled as simply pornographic in a few of the countries to which they are exported. However, such base commercial reasoning need not interfere with your decision-making at this stage of the proceedings.

And while the subject is to the fore, you will find that many of these comics provide an elementary grounding in various fields of wining and dining which you may well find useful later. They even run to articles on matters of general interest which you could usefully draw on as an aid to intelligent conversation. This however, comes later in the scheme of things. Back to the bedroom, then, and the naked you . . .

You will find, this being Britain, that on a great number of occasions which need not be even remotely formal, the venue of your choice will probably dictate the nature of your clothing, since we do not yet seem to have adopted the rather more relaxed attitude to this sort of thing currently nurtured by our American cousins.

The first time I ever went to the great US of A, fresh (although after 13 hours that's perhaps the wrong word for it), straight off the plane in Las Vegas, and all agog with excitement, I asked the cab driver where in town I could go, 'dressed like this'. The 'this' in question was shirt and jeans, with a bomber jacket to match. 'Son,' he said, looking over his shoulder rather inappropriately, since we were thundering down The Strip at not inconsiderable speed at the time, 'son, you can go to the best places in America dressed like that. All you've got to do is pay the bill.' This rather splendid attitude to dress has yet to pervade our tiny island, as anyone who has attempted to gain entrance to even the weediest local disco will testify. The trouble is, of course, that in America anyone can be a millionaire (and most of them seem to be) bringing untold wealth into the establishment. To be totally fair this air of enlightenment has reached certain quarters, mostly in our larger cities, but generally speaking you must still dress according to the nature of your destination.

The converse is naturally also true. You would look like a prize buffoon attending a race meeting at some vast and muddy field all done up in a velvet jacket and a pair of white spats, although you would certainly create an impression, not to say a stir.

In these hard and improverished times it is not the lot of the average mortal to possess vast sums of the green and folding with which to purchase a varied and extensive wardrobe to suit every occasion, at which point we should all be grateful to Moss Bros and similar. Do not underestimate the potential of these people; they can hire you an outfit to do anything from attending a Buck House Garden Party to skiing up the Matterhorn, thus saving you a fortune. Your own wardrobe therefore need contain no more than you need to navigate the main stream of life.

Although we have so far only spoken of extremes be aware that the points made apply to greater or lesser degrees at every level. While there may be no firm rules about dress for most things you do, and practically nobody will come forward to assist you in your choice, everyone will notice at once if you get it badly wrong, so it is most necessary to cultivate at least a few glimmerings of taste.

With the correct sense of occasion in mind, then, your next step must be to take that long, hard look at yourself. What you are looking for here is the extreme. Extreme good, and extreme bad. For starters, people with a more than pronounced beer gut should avoid tight jeans and slinky T-shirts. These things will conspire to produce what may best be described as an expectant bulge at the front. Whatever your opinions on the masculine nature of anyone who can successfully take on 14 pints of heavy a night without falling down more than once or twice, women will only find the inevitable consequences risible in the extreme. It is a feat of demonstrable complexity to perform Bodie and Doyle impressions with a vast gut swinging like a pendulum out front.

If you are in possession of such an item, or if you are unlucky enough to carry all your weight behind you, then it will behove you not to draw too much attention to the fact, whatever the dictates of fashion may prescribe.

By the same token you would do well to capitalise on your better features. If you sport a luxuriant growth of shining hair try not to wear too many hats. And if you are the proud owner of a vast chest, rippling with the sort of corded musculature which would make Luca Brazzi look like Noddy's hairdresser – don't conceal it. Modern-day skin-tight denims are likewise a very wondrous thing, providing you've got the legs for it. Not many men think about their legs in this way, but a great number of women think of men's legs in exactly this fashion. Long legs and a nice bum, when attached to a man, have much the same effect on women as do the female variety upon men.

And this is a big clue. Women, contrary to what you believe, and would most probably like to continue believing, do look at men as critically as you look at women. You don't like shabby, untidy women, do you? And there's no earthly reason to suspect that women are fond of tramps or those who resemble them.

Your wardrobe will contain a reasonable variety of clothes which will carry you through casual, semi-smart and formal occasions, then. All of these items will have been selected in order to show off your finer points and conceal those things of which you are most ashamed.

Unless you are colour-blind these garments will also have been chosen on a toning basis. That is to say you will not ever consider wearing a pair of garish orange trousers topped off with a lime-green sweatshirt and concealing a pair of fluorescent pink socks, despite what you have just seen on *Top of the Pops*. Many such combinations look wonderful on stage or on the box but will earn you little more than well-deserved laughter and insult in the saloon bar of The Three Ferrets.

On the contrary, you will have decided which colours suit you best (believe it or not your hair colouring or your eyes, even the tone of your skin, will probably dictate this) and opted for them. Enlist the aid of other people in this. Preferably enlist the aid of a woman, or women. They like giving advice of this nature, are flattered to be asked, and will respond well, even if you have never met them before in your life. Attractive girls working in shops, even attractive female customers, will suffice for this purpose. And if you don't know them now you might do by the time they've chosen the colour of your most intimate garments for you. It's always worth a try.

With this sort of help you will soon get the picture and be able to do it all by yourself. If you're lucky with the female opinion and assistance we've just been speaking of you may find that it's more entertaining and rewarding to continue looking helpless when confronted with a rack of clothes.

Now then. Since we know what's in your wardrobe now, and we know why it's there rather than some Hawaiian-style shirt dyed in colours visible only to bees, we can go ahead and choose our clothing for tonight with regard to our destination. There was a time when the nature of your dress would, to a goodly extent, have dictated the type of women you were likely to encounter. In such times smart operators would have reversed the procedure and dressed according to the type of women they were aiming for. Fortunately you need not worry about this sort of thing any more. There was an old saying: 'a cat may look at a King'. You've heard it before, no doubt. These days a cat may not only look at a King. A cool cat can make off with a princess, even if he is wearing jeans, so don't worry.

Just pick out the items you require from the wardrobe. You may do this in the happy and comfortable knowledge that you will look as good as you can do because you are a smart and sensible geezer, are you not? You will have had the foresight to ensure that the things in your wardrobe are all clean, won't you? Course you will, course you will. You're not the sort of bozo who will turn up anywhere in a jacket which bears the remains of your last meal (or is it something less appealing?) clinging to the lapel. You won't be wearing jeans or trousers which have spent the past fortnight jammed down the back seat of your car in order to silence that funny rattling noise you've been meaning to have fixed. And your shirt. That will be clean and well-ironed, I'm sure. All the very best toggery the fashion houses of London, Paris and New York have to offer will come to nought if you abuse it, use it for unspecified purposes the designers didn't even conceive of and then expect to wear it without anyone noticing.

Having said all that there are other, more subtle nuances to consider. I once went out for a while with a young lady who was absolutely convinced I was married, although this was not the case. Nothing would change her opinion on this subject for some time. Eventually she was forced to reveal the reasoning behind this strange and erroneous belief. Anyone, she said, whose shirts were that well ironed must have a woman tucked away somewhere.

There is much to be said for this eventuality. A great number of women nurture a strange desire to look after and fend for a man in everyday matters of this kind. Feminists tend to scorn the image of the little lady at home, washing and ironing, sewing on buttons etc, but the instinct still persists to a fairly high degree; nor is it the exclusive preserve of the more mature female. A lot of women will find the crumpled shirt, back-to-front sweater or unmatched socks strangely endearing. If you know that this is the nature of the female you are meeting there is no harm in allowing the faintest modicum of this sort of thing to creep into your clothing. But be warned. First, don't overdo it, otherwise you run the risk of being considered an out-and-out slob, and second, remember that this is a dangerous road with only one final destination. Unless you are a remarkably quick thinker and very fast on your feet leave this ploy well alone. Otherwise you will almost definitely meet a grisly fate at the hands of some jovial and avuncular vicar.

In general, and especially if your preferred image of yourself is of D'Artagnan rather than The Prisoner of Zenda, stay neat, clean and tidy. In the overall scheme of things you will meet with more success that way, and should survive long enough to enjoy it on a permanently repetitive basis.

Now you're almost ready for the off. Scrubbed clean, nattily attired, smelling, if not exactly sweet and still less like a tart's parlour, at least like one of the less offensive products of the perfumier's art, what's missing?

Not a lot, as it happens. Remembered to clean the teeth, did you? After all, you may be excessively fond of Jack Daniels or Theakston's Old Peculiar, but the chances are that not every woman in the world will agree with you. Worse still, you'll find that a great number of them don't actually like curry, especially not the three-day variety which must be kept in a specially-constructed, extra-deep bomb shelter. And peculiar as it may be, some women actively dislike garlic, for reasons known only to themselves. And although furious application of the latest fluoride-striped dental compound will not actually erase all traces of this sort of thing it will at least provide a reasonably efficacious barrier, at least until you get in really close. By which time it shouldn't matter that much anyway. And it will prove that you've tried.

At this point the world, though it may not be the

equivalent of your own personal variety of aphrodisiac shellfish, is definitely ready, and awaiting your arrival. More to the point, you're ready to take it on. Let's go.

Choose Your Targets

Beauty is altogether in the eye of the beholder
Lew Wallace, *The Prince of India*

It is quite conceivable that a great many women may resent the freebooting male of the species regarding them as targets, either collectively or individually. It is even more certain that feminists as a group will be decidedly bitter about it. Without wishing to approve or condemn such attitudes there is little doubt that most men and most women regard the situation which exists at present as remarkably similar to a hunt. There are only a few unusual instances to contradict the widespread belief that, all this being true, men are the predators.

This is a peculiar attitude for both parties to adopt. The only popular alternative to this is the 'cattle market' feeling prevalent among young ladies who are wont to populate discos and dance halls. In nearly every instance of this attitude the girls are angered by the feeling which this sort of event generates, and resent the implications.

The comparison between a cattle market and a disco is not, however, a particularly apt one. Cows, let's face it, are singularly unattractive animals with few redeeming features – unless of course you happen to be a bull. They are noticeably lacking in perspicacity of any sort, demonstrate hardly any perceptible signs of individual will and are, in the final analysis, of limited practical value. And as if that wasn't enough, there are few cows which evidence any sign of personal charm. Indeed, some of their habits are little short of revolting.

Cows do make regular appearances at cattle markets, though. In nearly every case known to science they are unwilling participants in such events, and I am assured by people who know about this sort of thing that almost all of them are conducted there contrary to their own earnest desires to remain elsewhere. Few cows, I believe, harbour any real ambition to become beefburgers, and the sight of red-nosed clowns in orange tartan jumpsuits is sufficient to induce panic in the breasts of even the most peaceful grazing herd in much the same ways as the smell of mint sauce frightens the life out of your average sheep.

Women in discotheques are an entirely different bucket of haddock. To begin with women are attractive, charming creatures, pleasing to the eye and comforting to the touch. They are all of them individualists in the extreme and demonstrate a firmness of purpose coupled with a devastating and unequalled ability to impose their will on others. In short there could hardly be two creatures less similar than cows and women.

Personal research into this subject has led to another inevitable conclusion which women may perhaps not relish overmuch; all the females I have spoken to in discos or what-have-you were all, without exception, present of their own free will. And not only had they all been given the option of not attending at all but most of them came of their own desire. They were there, you see, because they wanted to be.

This may not surprise you overmuch, but then you probably haven't been to some of the places I have. Some of them, and this is not a joke, are out and out toilets. Yet still the girls flock there. The cattle-market comparison doesn't really hold up, then, does it? And by pure coincidence at the same time as that loses credence, so also does the image of the predatory male.

It is a simple fact that discos are places of entertainment

whose principal contribution to civilised life is to allow the male of the species to mingle freely with the female in the hope that this social intercourse may well lead to the other kind. Knowing this to be true, large numbers of males go to discos. Large numbers of females go there too, and for exactly the same reasons, despite their frequent protestations to the contrary. And we may rest assured that any hunting which takes place there is of a strictly reciprocal nature, although men and women tend to go about it in rather different ways.

Your average *homo sapiens*, whatever the height or depth of his individual sapience, tends to arrive in the disco late, slightly intoxicated (since he cannot afford to get drunk once he's in there) and in the company of several friends. They will cruise round the outside of the dance floor, possibly alone but more probably together, until they spot a likely-looking bunch of women. They will all move onto the floor as a pack, bolstering each other's confidence, possibly mumble something like 'nnndance', with a casual and almost non-existent question mark at the end of it, and see how they progress from there on. This is the 'cloned' method of hunting and is the most frequently seen tactic. There are, of course, a few individuals who operate in an entirely different fashion, but they're bound to crop up again later and may safely be ignored for the present.

Women, on the other hand, behave entirely differently. The greatest effort for the female huntress is made before she gets anywhere near a discotheque, dancehall, pub, club, restaurant or bus stop but is still a procedure which involves just as much ritual as the male 'search and destroy' strategy.

Anyone with even a limited experience of women, in fact anyone who has met their own mother for more than a fleeting period, will already be familiar with all of this. Women spend hours in the bathroom. They are not performing natural bodily functions. They are washing all over, filing nails, plucking eyebrows, examining their reflection in assorted mirrors with an excessively critical eye, brushing their hair a thousand times in each direction and finally applying the equivalent of a week's wages of a production-line worker at Ford in assorted compounds to the most remote corners of their bodies. From here they proceed to the bedroom, in which place they spend an equal period of time. For the most part they will be climbing into garments, shrieking with horror and discarding them before performing the same actions with a different item of clothing. After a prolonged period of agony, which in all likelihood will have been punctuated by at least two hysterical outbursts and one short-lived resolution to consume a fatal dose of noxious poison, they will emerge. At this point they will be happy, smiling, attractive, even beautiful.

Never believe that women do not hunt men as aggressively as men hunt women.

Now that we are cognisant of all this we may safely return to our chosen purpose: selecting a target. If we are to treat all this as a sort of minor science, then I'm afraid we're rather lumbered with the terminology.

The first thing to consider here is yourself. This is of course an amazingly selfish attitude and doubtless one which you have (quite properly) been urged to abjure. But there's a time for everything, even selfishness. Now is the time. So put your conscience aside for a moment and examine your state of mind. What are you looking for? Unless you know the answer to this simple question you are sure to meet with a pronounced lack of success. You would hardly be surprised to lose a snooker match if you arrived at the venue in whites and clutching a willow bat, would you? So define your objectives.

It's quite possible that you have no objective save that of going out for the evening and having a good laugh, in which case you have little to worry about. Except the probability that you'll be doing the same tomorrow and the same again the next night and the next night . . . and so on.

If you do have a definite object in mind then it is quite likely that it will determine in advance the sort of place you should be going to. Let's begin with the basic and basest possible option, and assume that the only thing you have in mind is to get into a legover situation with a compliant female as rapidly and easily as you can. This is hardly the kind of desire which may be brought most readily to fruition in Granny Smith's Victorian Tea Rooms on a Sunday afternoon (although you should not ignore even the remotest of possibilities in moments of extreme desperation). No, even the slightest hint of common sense will allow a great number of similar truths to become self-evident, even without the assistance of Paul Revere.

What you will find most useful on occasions of this nature is probably the local charnel-house masquerading as a disco of sorts. There's at least one in every town, probably more, and you already know where it is. And it is precisely because it has this sort of reputation that people who are in need of the same thing you are searching for tend to go there. This applies just as readily to women as it does to men, fortunately, so there is less chance of a misunderstanding on either side.

Once there, select a lady who takes your fancy and try your luck. You may have to try it more than once, but if your local knowledge is as accurate as it should be you'll eventually attain your ambitions. A small allocation of caution is often advisable in this sort of place, mostly on account of the clientele. Pits of this nature are often frequented by the less civilised members of any community, which can be a drawback, and it's the geezers you've got to look out for. You will notice that many of them fit into the 'urban gorilla' mould. They wear shiny suits (outside it would be a sheepskin), very large gold ID bracelets, never smile and always talk out of the corner of their mouth without moving their lips. Their knuckles drag along the ground when they walk and they have impressively-dimensioned chests the width of an Olympic standard swimming pool. All too often they are accompanied by ravishingly beautiful women who are mostly left to their own devices once inside the building. The gorilla makes visual checks on her progress every couple of minutes and if you, in your naive innocence, appear to be encroaching upon his territory he will exact swift and painful retribution on the person of the offender. Despite the fact that the lady in question does not give out the 'occupied' signals either subliminally or by direct speech (indeed, she will probably do the exact opposite), which will complicate the issue from your point of view more than a little, the gorilla will be in no doubt that she is the weak and helpless victim of a stray aggressive male. This freeloader – you – will be the offender upon whose person the aforesaid retribution will be enacted.

Under such circumstances you have few options. The golden rule in all cases is simple: run. If you can't run – fly. If you don't he will kill you or (even worse) nearly kill you. As a last (and rather hopeless) resort you may care to try the 'Mohawk Indian Ploy', as developed by my fellow-coward Mark. Mohawks believed that mad people were the privileged innocents of life, possessed by the Gods themselves, and party to beautiful dreams and visions which less fortunate mortals were denied. Consequently they revered lunatics and would never dream of harming one. When the gorilla threatens, and there is no means of flight available, throw yourself to the floor, frothing and babbling like a nutcase. You never know, he might let you off . . .

It would appear quite possible that you are more inclined to frequent the more salubrious establishments in your neighbourhood as a result of all this, and who can blame you? While such an understandable air of caution may well preserve your bodily integrity it will leave you with another problem. You go to a higher-class establishment, then. The place is swarming with incredibly lovely ladies. In view of your singularity of purpose it is no surprise to find that *all* the women in the place are incredibly lovely. The hard part comes now. We know all about pills, emancipation, freedom of action, female sexuality and the rest of the deal. We are also clever enough to be aware that, of the few hundred girls in view, not all of them are at all desirous of jumping into bed with anyone, even Adam Ant himself, before the night is over. Of the small number who may be in exactly that frame of mind, thanks to a fortunate chain of circumstance, not all of them will be happy if the man in question is you. It would be exceptionally useful if you could just pick out those who are desirous of male company on an overnight basis in general, and then see if you fit the details of the bill afterwards.

Bad news all round, buster. There is absolutely no method of determining this information just by looking, and Utopia is dashed from your grasp yet again. This insurmountable obstacle is the precise reason why there are so many disappointed men everywhere. If you go out looking for a legover and nothing else there is only one sure way to get it. In addition to being rather expensive this solution is not without other attendant risks of an especially unsocial nature. And if you spend all your time looking at the women you meet simply as a source of physical gratification you'll wind up blind, spotty and, worst of all, alone.

The only thing you can do is go back to the beginning and just try getting to know a few girls who take your fancy. There is no shortcut round this and nor should there be, otherwise you would be denying the ladies their humanity and depriving yourself of a wide variety of pleasant experiences.

It is more than possible that in the course of such encounters you will bump into a lady who is more than keen to perform a number of superlatively pleasurable physical acts with you right off. This is coincidence and should be treasured. It is also the fruit of some kind of human contact with another person, however brief, which would probably not have arisen had you not accorded her the compliment of being regarded and treated as a human being and a woman rather than a pre-packaged product. Better still, the resulting union will in every case be far more gratifying and exist on a far higher plane than a frantic animal scrabbling in the back of a car with a girl whose name you didn't know to begin with.

What you must realise is that there is no instant formula for success on a Saturday night. There are a number of ways in which you can put that success within your grasp, but it depends on many factors, all of which will have to be working for you. So far we've only looked at a few of them.

One thing which you may often find will pay off at the

disco, and which could well lead you into a meaningful ongoing social interface with a person of the opposite wossname, sex, is boldness. This comes in several varieties, and we'll be coming to the important ones later. Most blokes only interpret boldness as that feeling of insouciance and light-hearted charm, that 'don't-give-a-damn' sensation which may be purchased in licenced premises all over the country in sixths of a gill, or more likely in pints. All of this has a place in your scheming and quite rightly so, but at present we are more concerned with making a bold choice when picking a target.

You're still in the disco, right? There's some wimp pretending to be a DJ up front. He knows all the right clichés – disco action, funk city, get down and groove and similar – but sadly doesn't have the brainpower or the vocabulary to join them together in an intelligible sentence. He repeats them endlessly, although not always in the same order, trying out a variety of mid-Atlantic accents all the time. He doesn't even stop when the records are playing and you know this is true because you can see his lips moving.

Since man is a social animal there are definite patterns of behaviour observable at all times, even here. Luckily for both of us we're only concerned with one thing, so we can forget most of it straight off. Just divide the audience into two halves. Forget about the geezers; dressed by Peter Robinson, haircuts by the same homosexual stylist down the road, all wearing Paco Rabanne aftershave and drinking Tia Maria and lemonade. Forget them. Concentrate on the women. Unless . . . no, couldn't be. Not you . . .? No. Look at the birds then. They're not without their own cloning routines, but as a rule girls seem to be much better at individuality and style when it comes to clothes than blokes. Even so you'll see the way it works. They tend to be of two kinds: those with a man, and those without. All previous comments about urban gorillas apply; 'Hey, broken-nose. Why you dancing with my girl?' You and I, of course, both know you don't have a broken nose. Yet. So ignore the ones who have a man in tow.

The others are the ones you want. Almost certainly they

will be in groups; even in today's liberated world women tend not to go to many places, even discos and dances, alone, which is surprising in view of the nature of their intentions, but still. And they need moral support from their friends just as much as men.

They dance with each other a lot, do women. In many parts of America this would be considered very strange. In fact it would be taken as an indication of decidedly Sapphic influences. Girls who dance together in the US tend not to meet too many smart men-about-town. In this country they dance together a lot. This is another part of the female hunting ritual which demonstrates a strange role-reversal which may in itself be a kind of perversity. Regular viewers of Beeb 2 will already know that almost all forms of life indulge in some form of courtship ritual, however slight. In many instances it is far from slight, involving complicated displays and dances designed to impress potential mates to the point at which they succumb breathlessly. The intriguing thing about all this is that out in the wild, as the pieces move on Mother Nature's checkerboard in the never-ending drama of life . . . well, anyway, it's the male who does all the fancy footwork. It's the male who puts on the display, showing off his extra-smart plumage or brand-new and highly colourful skin. Male peacocks – and as a rule male birds of most kinds – are the pretty ones and the females are the drab boring ones.

On the dance floor it's all different. It's the girls who have all the pretty feathers – the gold lurex T-shirts and skin-tight satin trousers – and who do the tripping of any light fantastic available in a blatant display calculated to induce sexual arousal. Very often they are highly successful in this and frequently succeed in attracting a great deal of attention from men. Next time you visit such an establishment have a look and you'll see that I speak with straight tongue.

Also, and now we get back to the point, you'll often see one, or maybe two, girls who excel at this sort of thing. Stunningly beautiful, immaculately dressed and with a highly developed sense of rhythm which will leave you speechless with admiration. Many of these girls also appear to have more joints in their bodies than your average contortionist and are capable of moving individual portions of their anatomy quite independently of the rest of it.

Strangely enough, all of this mobile sex-appeal may work against them at times. Because they represent what seems to be the summit of achievement for their species the overall effect is often the reverse of what they intended. A lot of blokes, while they may feel free to admire from a distance, and marvel at the astonishing number of moving parts which appear to be in full working order, will probably take their interest no further.

In truth, they're frightened off. They think that any lady as smart as this one must have heaps of geezers killing each other for a chance to pick up her handkerchief, or any other scented item of apparel which she may, from time to time, feel like dropping. She's an exceptional and special lady, and therefore requires an exceptional and special man. Whatever qualifications this god-like male needs it is certain that insurance clerks from Basildon won't have them, even if they do drive a jacked-up Cortina with furry dice dangling from the driver's mirror.

Since the bulk of men in discos are insurance clerks from Basildon (with or without jacked-up Cortinas) it is at once abundantly clear that aforesaid elasticated sex goddess is going to spend a high percentage of her life gyrating alone across the dance floors of the nation, awaiting the arrival of a knight in shining armour mounted on a white charger. Contrary to what the adverts would have you believe, managements of trendy disco-dance emporiums almost never admit white horses even if they are called Eric and accompanied by a human being.

Exceptionally attractive girls very often get asked to dance far less frequently than Miss Average. This is because a lot of men are yellowbellies. Next time you see a girl like that don't be put off, but try your hand. Chances are you'll be the first man who's spoken to her all night, and if you could play odds like that all the time you'd save a fortune on spot cream and aftershave.

It's quite possible that you may regard parties as offering

similar opportunities as discos, and in this you would be quite correct. However, you would be quite wrong to imagine that you should treat both venues in the same way.

The thing about parties is that, within limits, they are far more selective in content, consisting as they do primarily of a group of people who have all been invited. Although this will not mean that they are all known to each other everybody there will at least know someone in the room, who knows old George from down the road, and that's Fred who works in the garage, he's talking to Steve's (Steve's the one who drives those silly motorbikes in all weathers), Steve's wife, quite nice, John – he's an Estate Agent, you know, if you're ever buying – and the couple in the corner Bill and Doris, don't blame me he's my wife's brother not mine, and . . .

Commonality would be a good word for it. You could reasonably expect that a great proportion of people at such a gathering, while they may not come from the same background or even have been to the same sort of schools, will have many interests in similar fields. Half your work, therefore, is done for you, since this is the sort of thing you would normally have to allow for when choosing a target. More of that later. Even more of your work is done for you because of the selective nature of the event. Approaching strange girls in public places is often a bit like throwing down a gauntlet and challenging them to a duel of wits. At a party a great deal of this verbal swordplay will prove unnecessary because the lady will have at least lowered, if not altogether dropped, those of her defences which are designed to repel undesirable elements – insurance clerks from Basildon etc – at the earliest moment. This means that you shouldn't have to indulge over-long in the preliminary skirmishing; your presence at the same party as her establishes your credentials to an acceptable level, and as for your *bona fides* – well, it works wonders for those little buggers.

This form of streamlined social intimacy saves you a lot of time and may provide you with a much happier hunting-ground than your favourite disco, but it is not without its own particular pitfalls. These stem from exactly the same factors which accord all the benefits, are not very much more than amplified versions of your problems in discos and tend to come under the general heading of keeping your own doorstep clean. Although the sort of parties you go to will not be attended by the lowlife animals you may encounter at the seedier public establishments there will still be a number of women present who are attached to a man, not necessarily by marriage. Because a lot of conventions are relaxed a bit at parties, and because people feel more at ease in the company of people who may not be their peers and equals but who are more or less guaranteed 'safe', is often hard to spot which women are half of a couple.

Wedding rings assume double importance here as there is seldom any other form of evidence. Both sexes find it easy to flirt outrageously in this sort of environment. Body talk, eye-contact, physical contact or even embrace, overt sexual aggression while dancing – the whole set of rules goes right out of the window and you're in a very dangerous jungle. The possessive male won't be that far away, and his anger at being threatened is likely to be doubled or trebled by the sense of betrayal engendered because you've attacked on home ground, just when he thought it was safe.

Discreet enquiries are therefore essential before embarking upon any sort of adventure which you propose to press with serious intent, and this elementary precaution will allow you to reap all previously-mentioned benefits. You lucky thing.

Now then. Suppose you have travelled to this party or whatever, hung around for a while, drinking, socialising and enjoying yourself, and have usefully employed your idle moments and those brief forays into the kitchen, or wherever the booze is stashed, to conduct an in-depth but long-distance survey of what's about. Don't call you Hawkeye for nothing, do they? And suppose that even your piercing blue eyes (been practising your penetrating stare in front of the mirror again?) have failed to spot even one female who is not previously spoken for and could be considered remotely attractive? You could hardly blame yourself for writing the whole event off as a disaster and beating a hasty retreat home to your collection of pornographic videos, could you? Yet this is the measure of your determination and a guide to your true dedication to the cause.

Professionals will know the truth of all this, and will likewise be familiar with the 'Ugly Bardot' theory. In simple form it goes thuswise: if you are in a roomful of unattractive women then the best-looking (or least distasteful) one of the bunch must, for the purposes of that one evening, be regarded as the most beautiful woman in the world even if she looks like a Sumo wrestler's elbow. For that night she is Bardot, Miss World, whatever. If you've pulled the most attractive woman in the room you're doing fine.

Other advantages accrue. First, even if you don't go home alone, you still may not have to say you're sorry. Second, it can do wonders for a limp and fragile ego which otherwise might have suffered a further relapse. Third, and this is the most important bit, it is true to say that the most valuable things don't always come wrapped in the shiniest parcels. While physical appearance may be of great importance, especially on a short-term basis, there are other things to consider which may offer more splendid delights.

Ladies who are not accustomed to being swept off their feet by debonair Lotharios like yourself will in almost every case respond enthusiastically, and repay your attention a thousandfold. As you know by now, the care, attention and perhaps even admiration of a warm, responsive woman is an experience beyond compare. And since this sort of thing is a reciprocal chain reaction it is something you will both derive enormous pleasure from.

If luck is with you, and this enjoyable meeting advances to even dizzier heights as the night wears on, you will very likely be in for even greater surprises and delights. Two points obtain. If your companion is, as we surmised earlier, unused to this sort of thing then you could be about to reap a whirlwind. Having spent long evenings alone, perhaps, she may have had little opportunity to translate all the womanly desires and instincts, which she will possess just as surely as some nubile Lolita, into reality. But there's a good chance that she'll have read every novel, textbook and manual going, which means she probably knows things about physical gratification which would make an Archbishop kick a stained-glass window in, and which will almost certainly be well outside your own experience. You will now be presented with a superb opportunity to sample exquisite delights previously unknown to you, and also to learn volumes for future benefit. More than all this, further rewards await your delicate and sensual palate, and at this point it won't matter if neither of you have got past *Armpit* in The Encyclopaedia of Sex.

She's not used to supermen of your stature treating her like the most important person in the world, that much we know. She's responded joyfully, made you feel good, and you've spent some considerable time polishing each other's egos and flattering yourselves to death. She feels like Miss World. You feel like Casanova, Valentino. Truth is you're a pimply insurance clerk from Basildon and you look like Cyrano de Bergerac, but who cares? The trick with this is that it's all in the mind. If you feel beautiful you'll be beautiful.

If you do it right then I promise that as the evening progresses the lady in question will become more and more attractive. In part this is because she's feeling it and in part it'll be because she'll be developing a warm friendly personality before your very eyes. In extreme cases it may be because you're both drunk. But it doesn't matter. It works and that's all you need worry about.

Even if it all ends there you will find that your disastrous evening has turned out to be quite splendid. If it doesn't end there, and you repair to a private place together, then this lovely mood will persist and will be the source of pleasure and satisfaction which a hard-hearted union, no matter how skilful, can never parallel.

Ugly ducklings, let us never forget, turn into beautiful birds eventually. Also you would be surprised to learn just how many ugly ducklings turn out to have the heart and soul of a princess. And who knows, if they start kissing toads like you then perhaps you'll turn into a prince. Then again . . .

Parties, though they may not be the direct equivalent of Samuel Colt's Equaliser, are great levellers, bringing people of similar kinds together. Sociologists, and people like Willie Hamilton, would have you believe in a thing called the class structure. This is an intangible device which provides that insurance clerks from Basildon (with or without jacked-up etc) may not seduce titled ladies, or even females of great social standing and influence. For all practical purposes this is a hangover from Victorian times and no longer exists in its original form. As an example, you may care to recall the marriage of Princess Anne. The ITN news bulletin went something like this: 'Buckingham Palace today announced the engagement of Her Royal Highness Princess Anne, daughter of Her Majesty the Queen and His Royal Highness Prince Phillip, Duke of Edinburgh, to Lieutenant Mark Phillips, son of the Managing Director of a well-known pie and sausage company.' Yes, barriers are crumbling, although they have not totally vanished. It doesn't matter all that much anyway, since most people tend to move in circles which reflect their own position in society.

This is not as accurately delineated as it used to be, however, and a few proprieties need to be observed. For the most part the social barriers which our cosmopolitan modern world applies have less to do with accidents of birth, fortunate or otherwise, than with bank balances. At one time your income may reasonably have been expected to dictate both your social standing and, therefore, your level in Society. This is no longer true, and we find brain-damaged footballers (all doubtless over the moon with their new-found wealth) and grubby foul-mouthed pop idols rubbing shoulders with titled nobility and illiterate peasantry alike.

In either situation it is the folk idols of sport or music who rate the highest honours, the nouveau-rich industrialists (who are almost certainly in property development at the business end of a JCB) running a close second, with the merchant bankers and tax-lawyers coming in for a photo-finish third with BBC newsreaders. Aristocracy make a poor fourth.

While all this tradition has been turned on its head, a certain amount of new ideology has grown up. In so far as it concerns you it has only one effect. Although commoners may marry royalty with facility, insurance clerks from Basildon are prohibited from seducing Diana Ross or similar. Although the rules at the top have changed, the bottom line remains the bottom line. This is just as well, because you will all recognise Diana Ross next time you meet her in the bar of the Psychedelic Dragon, but you would have great difficulty in picking out the Duchess of anywhere by her face, still less by her dress.

You will know her at once when you speak to her, though, should you ever summon up sufficient (albeit ignorant) temerity, because she will freeze you with a glance. Hardly your fault, though, because waitresses in many a burger bar wear Gucci, St Laurent and whatever.

There is always the faint chance that such a lady may well be in search of excitement, reality, adventure with the proles and so on, not to mention a bit of rough. Although Connie's infatuation with the coarse and grimy person of the less-than-genteel Mellors is a warm and moving piece of literature (and also a lascivious piece of cinema), plus an extraordinarily attractive fantasy, it remains firmly in the realms of fiction.

It is unlikely in the extreme that any female member of the landed gentry will be looking through any bathroom windows in Basildon at the precise moment you are taking your monthly ablutions. Before you allow this to dash all your hopes and dreams know that it is far more conceivable that a begrimed and sweaty construction worker, fresh from the latest housing project and bearing the scars of a thousand near-fatal incidents involving powerful, throbbing machinery, will turn the heart and the head of a demure and attractive lady under the right circumstances. We have crossed swords with this dilemma before, and come to the conclusion that these instances are impossible to predict and almost impossible to, ah, engineer.

Which means that you will be wasting your time hanging about establishments generally frequented by demure women of superb breeding while covered in oil and/or brickdust, smelling like the Northern Outfall of an inner-city sewage system. Indeed you will be lucky to gain entrance to such establishments in the first place, and are very likely to be bounced down the road with a particularly virulent flea in your ear, if not actually on it.

Class barriers may be crossed, but only by accident. You can't predict it any more than you can spot the sort of lady willing to cross them. Just wait your turn is all.

All of what we have said so far is designed to apply mostly, if not completely, to situations in which you are running across the lady in question for the first time, maybe even the only time. It is entirely possible that you may be working on a long-term project. You may have already observed your target quite closely over a period of time, in which case you will be in possession of a great deal more information.

She will have made all the initial subliminal signals indicating availability, and your subsequent conversational research will have confirmed your initial impressions, in which case you may feel justified in taking a number of decidedly drastic steps, any one of which could end in disaster when faced with a quarry whose nature is unknown. This is all well and good, because once again you must remember we are playing percentages, and anything with low odds is a good bet. We'll come to long-term strategy later on, though.

What we should now be aware of is that there exists a great proliferation of opportunities, all different, and all of which require different handling, and we must now go on to consider the specifics of such handling.

Even though such variety is open to you it is more than certain that the sort of women you encounter will be your average woman, although perhaps not in the street . . . The percentages dictate that we should concentrate on this area since it is larger. The percentages also show that there are probably less people moving in the more exotic fields at either end of the social scale, which also works in your favour as long as you are perceptive enough to analyse the situation and choose the area which offers the most fruitful opportunities. Each place, remember, and each day, as well as each woman, must be regarded individually, and treated on its particular merits.

Having once decided on all this, and reached firm conclusions about the nature of your surroundings, made a well-reasoned choice of likely target, read all the signs and decided that the coast is clear for a fair passage to whatever destination you have in mind, the time is ripe for action.

At this point your success or failure hangs on perhaps a single word, perhaps the first one you utter. Unless you are at a wife-swapping party already, a cheery 'do you come here often?' will wipe you off the map at once. Nor can you besiege your target like Hitler's Blitzkrieg going through The Low Countries.

Other conversational gaffes may be more obscure and subtle, but will still result in your being sunk without trace. I am much indebted to David Niven's excellent work, *The Moon's a Balloon*, in which he described a meeting between the colossal beauty of Lauren Bacall, film star, and the colossal wealth and breeding of the Shah of Persia, heir to the Peacock throne and similar. As their dance together ended the Shah, a gentleman of immense tact, remarked that, 'You dance divinely, Miss Bacall.'

'You bet your ass, Shah,' replied the lady.

Clearly this sort of thing will not do, and certain proprieties must be observed.

Know Your Lines

Well said: that was laid on with a trowel
William Shakespeare, *As You Like It*

You've read the fairy tales. You may even have been lucky enough to catch the *Python* version of them on stage. In any case the theme's the same. There's this King, you see, and his daughter, the Princess, is very beautiful although only 18. She is also, by coincidence, single. The King is getting old and frail, though, and knows he will soon die. If peace and order are to continue in the Kingdom after his death he must have a successor. Since he has no son the Princess must marry soon. All kinds of freeloaders and fortune hunters, including the upper crust, who are trained to excel in these things, offer themselves as potential husbands. Being Prince Consort is not only cushy, it's quite well-paid. The King is not silly, though, and sets them all very difficult tests in order to find out whether they really love the Princess and will thus be Good Kings, of if they're just after the money. Course they're all after the loot, and who can blame them, so they all fail. Then along comes Leofric. Well-born, but not rich, handsome in the extreme but a bit soft on account of being dropped on his head while still a baby. He offers his hand in marriage to the Princess. The King says he must take a test. 'Why?' asks the pleasant, but dimwitted Leofric. 'Because she's a fucking Princess, that's why,' roars the King.

That was hundreds of years ago. Not every girl was a Princess, even then, although all their fathers thought they were, and still do. But their would-be husbands still had to pass some sort of test. Valiant knights in shining armour used to knock seven kinds of evil out of each other in order to prove how much they loved some Lady or other, and the girls were dim enough to accept this mindless slaughter as proof of endless devotion.

Fortunately this barbaric practice seems to have more or less died out over the years, possibly due to the low survival rate of the participants, maybe thanks to the encroaches of what we are now pleased to call civilisation. It is no longer necessary to hack limbs from your best friend in order to get wed, though duels over the hand of some dishy female were reasonably commonplace until comparatively recently, even if they weren't *de rigeur*.

With hand-to-hand combat safely out of the way it is still a fact that you will have to pass some sort of test in order to impress your chosen love. Chocolate adverts on the box will confirm this if you are in any doubt.

Since it is no longer feasible, still less desirable, to risk disfigurement in this cause modern society has fiendishly devised a series of lesser tests for you to take on in your quest for romance. Ladies, whatever their apparent gentility, still find great pleasure in seeing men prove themselves in worthy causes. Like wooing, for example. Luckily they do not expect them to die trying. These lesser tests, which are of a distinctly ongoing nature (and in the event of marriage will last a lifetime, you have my word on it), are of such minor fatal potentiality that they are now part of accepted courtship rituals in the Western world. As you blaze your trail through the drawing rooms (and hopefully other sorts of rooms) of the female world you will encounter many such tests. Forewarned is forearmed, they say, and you will learn to recognise them for what they are as we explain them and then deal with them accordingly. All in good time.

For now we are concerned with the immediate situation.

You have prepared yourself carefully for this evening's quest, and taken account of all the information at your disposal. Clean, presentable, in the right place at the right time, equipped with maximum intelligence concerning the disposition and location of the quarry, you're beginning to sound more like a soldier every minute. This is very right and proper too, because if you wish to carry the day in the battle of the sexes that's exactly what you'll have to be. At this moment you are ready to go over the top, so to speak. You are about to face your first test, and to do this you will need courage. If you are devoid of this commodity, or even if you appear to have temporarily mislaid it – take heart. Only cowards win medals. The unafraid are too stupid. It will do you no harm at this stage of the proceedings to compensate for the lack of the natural bravery by artificial means. Have a drink or two, smoke a hundred cigarettes, whistle a happy tune, whatever suits you best. Now for the first test: conversation.

Make no mistake about it, this is going to be a test. You have come here, wherever it is, with the express intention of engaging the enemy. And she, contrary to your fond imaginings, will be in no doubt about your purpose. Women are not stupid, whatever else they may be. However discreet your scrutiny of the opportunities may have been, she will have already spotted you and noted your intentions. She's hunting too, remember, and is every bit as alert and keyed up for the chase as you are. At this point you may comfort yourself with the knowledge that she knows as little about you as you do about her. As yet, she doesn't know if she's dealing with a prize wimp or one of the crowned heads of Europe any more than you do.

Unless, that is, you've been acting like a wimp already, without even opening your mouth. Go to a disco a couple of times and watch it happen for yourself. Geezer strolls in, casts an eye about the place, wanders over to the bar and cops a drink. Then he begins a slow circuit of the place, checking out all the possibilities. Somewhere in this process he spots his chance. You'll see it happen. He stops his circuit a while, lingers in the area, flicks her up and down with his cool appraising stare, and moves on. If he finds nothing better he'll come back and repeat the process. He'll check for rings and attendant men, suss the table she's on for pints of beer (dead giveaway, that), and if all meets with his approval – he'll do nothing. He'll think it over, have another drink or three, work himself up to it and finally approach the lady. Usually on the dance floor, usually right after the DJ has announced an imminent selection of slow smoochy jobs, usually with a minimum of words.

It happens all the time and it's so predictable you could win money betting on it. Women, not even women in discos, are not stupid. This we know. Furthermore, they are much more familiar with this routine than you or I will ever be. If we can spot it then we would be stupid in the extreme to imagine that women can't. The woman in question will have clocked this bloke from the first minute. And all the time he imagines he's been sizing her up in that cool way of his, assessing his target and deciding when to strike, she's been watching him. She can read his subliminal messages as well as he can read hers. Better, in fact, because he doesn't know he's being watched and she does. By the time he finally gets into action the chances are she'll be so bored she'll tell him to naff off. Even if she doesn't she will have already summed him up as a wally, not worth the time of day, still less her valuable intentions.

The message here is plain. Actions speak louder than words, so act. Don't just stand there, do something. If you're reading the lady properly, and by now you should be, then you will know the minute she marks you out for what you are. That is the moment at which you must act. Not two hours later, but right away.

In you go then. But remember she knows what you're about. At this stage neither she nor any other woman feels any antipathy to you unless you are so ugly you'd frighten a buffalo, in which case God help you. You and she share similar aims, ultimately, perhaps even immediately. You wish to decide whether she will come up to your particular set of specifications. She wants to know if you meet hers. This is where the tests start coming.

The first one will be in progress the minute you start walking towards her. Women, for entirely unpredictable reasons known only to certain species of wildlife, can get really funny about some aspects of posture. The way you walk, the way you sit, anything. I know one girl who fired her boyfriend because she couldn't bear the way he placed his feet when he walked. There is no explanation for this, and no way to overcome it. You may well fail the first test without even knowing you've entered for it. If you fail then this is one of those occasions when you should accept the blows of fate with a shrug and push off to greener pastures.

If you pass then the next obstacle will present itself the minute you open your mouth. This has no connection with the tone or quality of your voice, although squeaky jobs are a drawback in the same way that deep husky growls are an advantage. Again, there's nothing you can do about that. Ignore women stupid enough to let a high-pitched squeak come between them and the caring, considerate, virile person who lurks beneath.

If all is well in this sector it will be the content of your speech which will most affect the results of this test. Once again it is environment which will most decide the nature of what you say. Breezing up to a coroneted Duchess at the Hunt Ball, with one finger buried in your left nostril, and saying 'D'y'wanna dance, tart?' is a tactic unlikely to meet with a great deal of success. Rules of this nature are simple and glaringly obvious. Don't ask amputees to dance, don't offer to buy drinks when the bar's closed and never offer policewomen drugs.

What the lady is looking for from you is some indication that you are witty, charming, intelligent and interested in her. This sounds like a particularly tall order, especially if you possess none of these commendable traits. Originality is the best alternative to all of these. If you come out with some hastily-mumbled platitude she's heard a thousand times before it may not mean that she'll rule you out of her life straight away, but it will mean you'll have to do better in the next round, so try not to get behind on points. You've got to be at least as good as the last chap who approached her, preferably better.

Once again this is easier if you know a bit about her, but you don't, so you're stuck. Still, make sure that you've read her properly from afar, though, and see if you can make out what sort of person she is, and therefore what she's most likely to respond to. Try to capitalise on your situation. You could be really lucky and be in the area at the precise moment she spills her drink. Don't hesitate, but get straight in with a cloth. A clean cloth. Mop her up, offer advice – cold water to rinse her gown, whatever, sympathise and then get her another drink. Don't just stand there sniggering into your beer.

If she's fighting for a place at the bar – go to her aid. Get her round in for her, or at least carry her drinks. Get a tray off the barman. It doesn't really matter what it is, just do something useful. In this way you will clearly demonstrate that you are a resourceful capable male, more than ready to deal with life's little upsets, take disaster in your stride and generally smooth her path before her.

Be careful with this, because it is quite easy to overdo it without even realising, and all you will demonstrate then is that you are a prize creep fit for little more than she may reasonably expect from a waiter in a halfway decent restaurant. The same naturally applies at parties. By all means whizz to the rescue when she's trying to reach across the table for that delicate morsel of caviare. Carry her overloaded plate for her. If she's having trouble managing food and drink while standing – help her. Don't offer to hold her wine glass and talk yourself into the role of glorified hatstand; show her how to cope (if you know) or clear a space on a convenient flat surface so that she can put her glass down. When she's finished eating by all means relieve her of the empty plate. Don't be a dummy and waltz off with it never to return until summoned; get her a fresh drink at the same time so that you have automatic re-entry into conversation.

If she's looking for the bathroom – tell her where it is. Don't show her. This is a sensitive activity and even though you may have been brought up to believe that it is polite to open doors for women they will not relish being ushered into toilets by obsequious strangers. Tell her where it is and offer to guard her glass – or better still refill it – against her return.

Anything of this nature will achieve two things. It will make your initial contact with the lady, and make it easily and naturally, and it will also get you past the first test and lower her resistance even if only by a tiny amount. Assisting women in tiny ways such as this used, long ago, to be such an accepted way of making this initial contact that it was not unusual for women to drop small items – handkerchiefs and so on – in the hope that the man they had taken a fancy to would pick it up and return it. This was a direct invitation cloaked in sufficient etiquette to make it deniable later on should the need arise. While few men regard the prospect of picking up damp Kleenex from a beer-soaked floor with any relish, and not many women would actually welcome the return of such an offensive article, the game remains the same.

It is a regrettable truth that these opportunities will not always present themselves, and you will still be left with the task of making that first contact without the benefit of any such help. In this event there is no alternative but to make sure that you present yourself as agreeably as you can and we are consigned once again to the opening line. Like first impressions these few words will count for a great deal and may even colour the final outcome of your encounter regardless of what transpires later. You will find that magazines – especially women's magazines – frequently produce useful lists of things about the battle we are all engaged in. They will be of the '100 things women like about men' variety and are generally immensely entertaining. More remarkably they will all come out with a different set of results, which means that you're no better off than you were before you read them. If you are silly enough to believe them utterly, that is. Used as a general guide they are often most illuminating.

One constant factor which emerges from this sort of survey, and is always in the top five, if not number one, is this. Women do not, as a rule, believe that looks are everything. One thing they do all seem to rate very highly is humour. What this means to you is gratifying. Although all previous remarks about first impressions and physical appearance must still apply, you can, once you get the opportunity, relegate your hook nose and warts to a back seat if you have the charm and intelligence to overshadow them. It is in this way that portly gentlemen with more chins than they actually require can often form rewarding relationships with desperately sexy women you would have expected to see in the company of slim-hipped superstars.

All of which is nice to know but of no practical value at this stage. Sad to say, you will never develop a sense of humour if you don't already own one. You can't be taught this sort of accomplishment. Most humour stems from originality these days. It used to be banana skins and fat old ladies, but it's a bit more sophisticated in the eighties. You can't be taught originality either, as it happens, but you can school yourself to avoid the obvious clichés, and to climb out of the most densely-populated ruts.

In a disco it's dead easy to approach a girl and ask her to dance. You just way 'Would you like to dance?' This is a workable method which produces results on a continuing basis and which the lady is quite likely to appreciate. She knew what you wanted when you walked up to her anyway, did she not? The same effect is possible in many other ways. Some of them are cleverer than others, some will appeal to one woman and not another. If she doesn't like your sense of humour or your attitude then the chances are she won't like you either. In all probability you won't fall desperately in love with her, so it would do no harm to elaborate upon even the most basic of conversational gambits in order to save time later. Unless you have only the one object in mind and she has the body you want, in which case play it safe. If you're looking for more than that then apply your own personality to opening lines.

There are huge avenues open to you here, and you would do best to find your own lines rather than nick mine since it is unlikely that our sense of humour will always coincide and it's you who wants to seduce the woman, not me. Guidelines may be useful.

Don't be fooled into thinking that something you say is so witty and original she'll be unable to resist you. There are a limited number of opening lines and most women have heard them all, in one form or another, before. It's like barmaids and waitresses. It is almost impossible, if not completely so, for any man to approach an attractive barmaid with a line she's never heard before unless he's lucky enough to catch her on her first night. I don't care what happens, don't care if the roof falls in or he wins a hundred grand on the pools. Whatever he's got to say, she's heard it all before, and probably twice. The more pithy comments or requests she will very probably have heard ten times already since the pub opened two hours ago.

While this may seem to present an obstacle of truly impressive dimensions you should not allow it to deter you. Even girls who have to listen to chat-up lines all their working life are still flattered by attention and will still be pleased you tried, though they may not admit it, even to themselves. Women – all women – like compliments, and sexual attraction is beyond doubt a compliment.

You're still trying to be a bit different, here, remember, and impart your unique and individual stamp to what's happening around you, perhaps with a dash of humour thrown in at the initial stages to test the water. Forget 'Would you like to dance?' Try 'May I have the pleasure, or would you rather dance?', but only in the right circumstances. This is unlikely to be well received by a brainless 18-year-old dropout from the Barry Manilow fan club. It's unlikely to work that well in very many discos, really. This is a moment at which your environment could prove to be critical. There is a convention which says that all discos shall be places with subdued but flickering lighting, decorated almost exclusively in violent shades of red and crimson and full of plastic ferns and chrome-plated furniture which is so uncomfortable that you are unlikely to sit on it for very long. They are all highly-skilled exponents of the art of muzak, and have taken it to extremes, playing music from record all of which is entirely indistinguishable from its predecessors and successors. In order to conceal this fact they play all of it at an excruciating volume which renders convesation impossible. As a side-effect it makes your teeth itch and your ears bleed, and may also induce madness in a few individuals during certain phases of the moon, but that's another story altogether.

In so far as it concerns you there is only one fact to be taken into account from all of this. You are wasting your time making with smart lines of chat in places where you have to shout so loud in order to be heard that your tonsils jump out of your mouth every time you breathe out. Now is the time to keep it short, sharp and simple.

'Do you wanna dance, tart?'

'Yeah, all right.'

'Good. Mind if I have your seat?'

In these conditions it will not matter if your opening chat is as subtle as a smack in the chops with a brick; your best work must be done later, once you are out of the disco and safely removed to a place with more forgiving acoustics. While in the inferno (and also at other moments) it will be valuable if your first words are reasonably specific, such as inquiries about dancing or drinking. Anything other than this, in addition to being more complex than circumstances allow, will also mean that your lady will either think you are a moron or will provide you with a noncommittal answer which will leave you no better off than before. Thus questions like 'Hey, babe, what's occurring?', quite apart from being so far over the top they become a source of hilarity to all those unfortunate enough to be subjected to them, invite responses like 'Nothing.' You are now the poor bastard who's got to follow up fast. So being direct, far from doing you harm, will actually work to your advantage.

Don't be too direct, though. Walking up to complete strangers of the opposite gender and asking them to come back home with you can lead to trouble. There are rumours to the contrary which you may have heard. They concern a bloke – someone's brother, best friend, mate of a cousin's step-brother twice removed – who makes a practice of

approaching women in discos with the same blunt question. In blunt, direct terms the question constitutes an invitation to participate in sexual congress whose energetic nature has so far been unequalled in the experience of the young lady thus approached and probably unsurpassed for star quality in the history of the world. This bold inquisitor of legend is always (with startling convenience) asked the same incredulous question; 'Don't you get your face slapped a lot?' 'Yes. But I also get laid a lot too.'

Mathematicians may care to calculate the odds involved in this ploy. It seems quite feasible that, if you're only interested in playing percentages for the sake of it, this technique may well work in your favour. Sooner or later you're bound to get a favourable result, and over a period of time you should get many results. But it does mean asking the same question over and over again on numerous occasions. It is probably necessary to visit vast numbers of discos or similar watering-holes on the same night before any degree of success is realisable.

To date nobody will vouch for the efficacy of this method from personal experience, and although the odds do seem to be somewhat appealing there are few people coarse and insensitive enough to try it on a regular basis. As a rule one good loose backhander from an enraged female is enough to bring the plot to a hasty and painful conclusion.

While discos and other loud places have the distinct advantage of existing for a singularity of purpose which facilitates your ambitions it is quite clear that they also suffer from a number of drawbacks. Volume is not the least of these, nor is it confined exclusively to a few places. We have already established that parties present fewer problems since your presence there serves the same purpose as your opening line in a disco, but they can also be loud as well. With luck the loudness will be confined to but a single room, and other, quieter, rooms will be provided for you to make closer acquaintance with ravishingly attractive women.

In this circumstance your conversation will be most important; you are at once placed in the same situation as if you had escorted a lady from a disco, without the advantage of knowing that she is there on your sole account and that you have already gained a great deal of ground. You have, in effect, passed the first test in either situation and are now approaching the second. This is stiffer than the first, and much more important.

Your entrée at a party may consist of one of several opportunities we have already considered, or it may be due to a straightforward approach with a conversation-piece. 'My name's Saint George. Haven't we met before?' This requires a sense of humour in the lady if it is to meet with any degree of success. If such a refinement is lacking you could well end up with a kick in the teeth, so be cautious. On the other hand, something like 'You look like my first wife', may be better. As long as you get the correct response – 'Oh. How many times have you been married?' Which leaves you with 'Never'.

Nice work if you can get it, but don't expect every woman in the world to play straight man to your comic act without the benefit of the script. You may find that contrived routines of this kind will work best if you operate with a friend who can feed you with the right lines on cue. He will need to be able to maintain a deadpan expression throughout this scene, which is something that beomes increasingly difficult if you work it more than once or twice.

In similar vein you will find that 'What's a girl like you doing in a nice place like this?' and witticisms of similar ilk will depend very largely for their success on the nature of the recipient, which you have already been well-advised to check out in advance unless you relish the prospect of having your face temporarily closed for repairs.

This may be an opportune moment to ponder over the regrettable instance of the knock-back, should such a thing occur. In all truth it will occur far more often than you succeed in luring a woman into your bedchamber unless you are very famous, very wealthy or amazingly good-looking, in which case I trust you will meet an early and painful fate.

The bulk of us will all get the elbow sooner or later, probably sooner and not always politely. As we have observed before this is only to be expected and should not be allowed to deter or discourage. When the order of the boot is administered you should take care to ensure that it has been properly done. Remember we are dealing with women intent on testing our mettle, and the 'hard-to-get' nonsense is a substantial portion of the female armoury. This is not an invitation to pursue unwilling girls home in the dead of night in an effort to convince them that you really care, nor is it a suggestion to drive them crazy with repeated invitations to dance or have a drink or anything else they've already refused 200 times. But it is always worth trying to overcome that first, polite refusal. This tactic may pay off quite well. If it doesn't it will provide you with a chance to ensure that it is the boot you are being given rather than another one of those annoying little tests.

In the event that it is indeed the boot you should fall back with honour. Do not be tempted to indulge in grubby displays of histrionics or little fits of pique. Depending on the manner in which the boot is administered you may feel that honour requires a certain display of character. If this is so try to keep it subtle and maintain your dignity at all costs.

'Do you want to dance?'

'Not with you, you parrot-faced wassock.'

'Oh. I suppose a knobbing's out of the question then?'

Do not descend into the depths of vile insult and personal disparagement even if she does, otherwise you will attract a great deal of attention to yourself. At best this will considerably reduce your chances with the other ladies present and at worst it will, in public places, guarantee the attention of those ferocious gents known as bouncers, whose sole pleasure in life comes from tearing the arms and legs off poor sods like you. Discretion need not always be the better part of valour. Come to that the two things seem to bear little or no relationship to each other whatever. But it won't hurt you to cultivate a modicum of healthy fear.

It is possible that all of this may have combined to present a fairly unhealthy picture of the situation which need not be all that accurate. Do not form the impression that meeting women is an ordeal slightly akin to unarmed combat with a fully-armoured Samurai warrior, because this is far from the truth. There are extremes in every walk of life and it is mostly these we have been dealing with. Repetition is often dull and boring but sometimes useful, and reminding you that most women are not aggressive Amazons anxious to emasculate every man they meet will do no harm.

Most women are jolly nice people, dying to meet someone wonderful like you. They are unable to deny their own nature no matter how hard they try and will still act like women when confronted with a man; all those clichés about fluttering eyelashes and saying 'no' when they mean 'yes' or 'maybe' when they mean 'you try and stop me' are clear exaggerations of the truth. The truth is still there at the bottom of it all and never forget it. We may dignify all the thrust and parry with the general heading of courtship rituals or any other suitably descriptive phrase, but it wouldn't do for you to take it all too seriously, especially since most women look on it as something of a game. Which is more or less what it is. But only in these early stages. If your relationship progresses further then the time will come when it will cease to be a game in her eyes and will suddenly become deadly earnest. She will not tell you in advance that this is happening; she will expect you to guess, which is something you haven't got a chance of doing. There is nothing to be done about this, so there is no point worrying about it.

While it's still a game you may simply relax and enjoy yourself. The chances are that in doing so you will increase your chances of success many times over. Women possess a strange quality known only as intuition. You may look this word up in a dictionary if you wish but it will be of no use to you at all. Feminine intuition is a random description of an ability far beyond the proper definition of the word. Compared to feminine intuition telepathy, ESP, clairvoyance and palmistry pale into insignificance. Compared to the blinding revelations which afflict women all the great seers and prophets of history can only perform feats equivalent to predicting that if today's Friday tomorrow will be Saturday. This does not indicate that women can pick

Derby winners in advance, or even be of much value filling in a pools coupon, so don't start getting excited. Almost all of these supernatural powers are concentrated in the field of human response, which means that most of them know what you're up to all the time. Forget all that garbage about working late. Even if she says nothing at the time she'll know if you're lying; maybe she won't know what you were doing, but she'll definitely know what you weren't doing.

You might think that this doesn't concern you; after all, the greatest intimacy you and she have so far shared is probably limited to a financial transaction involving staggeringly minute quantities of alcohol at a vastly inflated price. But it does concern you a great deal, and relates to previous suggestions about enjoying yourself.

Tell you a secret. All this chatting up nonsense, smart one-line gags, smooth sophisticated banter about the Dow-Jones Index, whatever technique you employ, doesn't matter a damn. There's only one thing that matters and that's your state of mind. Boldness, confidence, call it what you like, it's that which makes the difference.

You want proof, I give you proof. It works on two levels, this, so two kinds of proof. Remember Karen? If you don't you haven't been paying attention so go back to the beginning and start again, I'm going to be asking questions later. After the foul-up in that direction you may recall that we left an ignorant and innocent 16-year-old hotfooting it to a place where many girls could be found under one roof in circumstances which would provide an atmosphere congenial to arranging close acquaintance.

In those deprived years of the late sixties few such places existed, even in enightened London, so it was make the most of a bad job and make do with the dubious pleasures available in the Top Rank Suite. These places, for those who missed them, were cavernous, impersonal structures large enough to land light aircraft.

As a newcomer I followed the elementary precaution of watching what happened. I was, if you recall, stupid, young, unskilled and scared half to death of the whole thing. I had no reason to believe, at that time, that this fear was in any way unusual. Until arrival at the Suite. There, all these blokes were just strolling up to women, speaking to them, with perhaps a laugh and a smile and then going off to the dance floor, strolling off to the bar or just strolling off.

How could they do that?

What were they saying? What could they find to laugh about so soon? How did they phrase their requests? Didn't they mind being refused? *All* the girls seemed to like *all* the blokes who spoke to them. Since it was unlikely that all the girls liked all the chaps it meant that the men could tell at a glance when women liked them, or how else did they always get a good result? Unless they knew some magic word or phrase which had not yet been vouchsafed to yours truly.

Careful study – prolonged observation and casual questioning during conversation with a few mates – revealed, eventually, the truth. There was no magic phrase. There was no way to tell if a woman liked you simply on the basis of a brief visual examination conducted in half-darkness at a range of 20 feet. There was, however, a trick to it. Confidence. Just act like all the women you speak to are already much enamoured, and act like you expect a positive result, and nine times out of 10 you'll get one. That's all there was to it.

It's a bit nerve-wracking at first, but you soon find out that it works. Fact is that the girls had gone there to meet blokes, wanted to dance, and would give almost anybody a fair crack of the whip. You can afford to be confident, because the odds are in your favour.

Even more convincing proof that confidence is a vital factor came later in life. It has, over a period of time, become fairly obvious that life can be a bitch. It was Spike Milligan who correctly observed that if life is a game of cards then some bastard is cheating. I have noticed a pattern in this. It seems that all the time I have a woman in my life on a more than passingly regular basis strange things happen. Without fail I bump into lots of women in the normal everyday run of things. In pubs, restaurants, wine bars, trains, anywhere. It has become plain on loads of occasions that many of these ladies are decidedly interested, if not actually available, even though I may have done nothing to bring this situation about. In fact it's generally a complication I don't need. These opportunities are always presented at moments when they are least required and are thus consigned to the file marked 'Under different circumstances . . .'

It is also clear that in moments of prolonged solitude and celibacy the most strenuous and devious attempts to procure companionship, whether on a temporary or semi-permanent basis, are doomed to ignominious failure. It's only when you give up hoping and trying that something works out.

At this juncture it is clear that confidence is vital. With a girlfriend somewhere in the background security is offered. The male ego is much boosted by the knowledge that someone somewhere thinks he is charming and handsome, a giant among men. Because she ignores his acne and his bad breath so does he. He may smell a bit, but he has a heart of gold and is an intrepid slayer of dragons. Because he feels attractive he *is* attractive, and not only to the girl in the background, but also to loads of others. He could pick up loads of women if he wanted to, but the timing's all wrong.

Bereft of all this comforting support the man feels ugly and unpleasant, and even when he tries his hardest to be charming he will possess, in the eyes of the ladies he is trying to charm, all the appeal and desirability of a rotting log. He is as exciting as a bowl of dirty dishwater, and his efforts are doomed to disaster.

Confidence is everything then, and not only because of the effect it has on the psychology of the man. This is where the miracle of feminine intuition comes into play. No matter what you say, no matter how witty and charming you may be and no matter how well you may conceal your inner doubts there is little prospect of the true state of things escaping the lady you are confronted with. She will not perceive any special signs, nor need to look deeply into your eyes. She won't need to read your palm or gaze into any crystal balls. She will just know, and there's no escape from it.

This matters little at times when you are on top of the world, because it will work greatly in your favour. But when you have been alone, deprived of the pleasures of feminine companionship for ages, and are just on the verge of suspecting you will never sample such delights again – that's when intuition will strike you yet another cruel blow. The circle is vicious, no doubt about it, and the effects are compound. A few really serious setbacks and you will be convinced that you're uglier than Charles Laughton in his make-up and as charming as an angry rattlesnake. Quite soon you will begin to believe that your Granny was right, and it does make you blind, stupid and ugly, and you may even start appreciating the finer characteristics of sheep and other furry animals with more relish than was previously the case.

All the time this continues the problem will intensify. Every woman you approach will detect an air of desperation about your person and spot that hunted look in your eye. Your eagerness to succeed will be the very thing which prevents you doing so.

Now is the time to remember the plus points. Refusals and lack of success are not only to be expected, they are vital. Otherwise how else will you appreciate to the full your moments of success? You can't enjoy being rich unless you know what it's like to be poor. Rebuild your own confidence. Write down on a sheet of paper all the things you've got going for you. If after two days the paper is still blank then remember that although it is highly explosive, North Sea Gas is not poisonous. Casting yourself from bridges or high buildings, or natural edifices of a precipitous nature is more traditional anyway. Remember to leave a note; not only will this make the task of the authorities so much easier, it will also give you a chance to pen heart-rending epigrams in the classical style of 'goodbye, cruel world' and ensure that everybody knows who to blame for the whole rotten mess.

Should natural cowardice preclude your taking the honourable way out you should return to the fray as casually as possible. Try not to be desperately keen. Don't resort to begging and pleading. Some women may like to see men cry, but not enough to go to bed with them out of pity.

Good hunters, once they have set their traps, walk off and leave them, allowing the quarry to become ensnared at its leisure. They do not, having dug a deep pit, go out and capture animals and then hurl them bodily into the abyss.

Bide your time, in conversation. By all means go to places where many women will be found. Lay out lines of bait and wait until it is taken before you reel in. Fishermen who constantly check their hook catch nothing, because it is never in the water when it should be. They succeed by being in the right place at the right time and then by patience. You will catch nothing by main force, so don't try.

Be grateful that nature has so arranged things that everything is in your favour. Secure in this knowledge you can afford to be relaxed and casual, you can afford to take pleasure in the game. There is nothing more attractive than someone who is an individual in his own right, is happy with life as he finds it and is confident enough to make the most of any opportunity without stamping his feet in anger when women refrain from swooning at his approach. Manic depressives cloaked in an air of gloom and despondency, sporting their own personal black cloud, and with the general air and demeanour of a perverted fiend accustomed to slinking about in the shrubbery bordering the ladies' lavatory in public parks are seldom regarded with great favour.

Perhaps a piece of hitherto unpublicised information will cheer you. Not many people realise that 50 percent of married couples are women. No one, not even an insurance clerk from Basildon, could believe that these ladies have entered the state of Holy Matrimony against their will; no, they must surely have co-operated quite willingly. And it is more than probable that the single ladies you encounter will be just as willing to co-operate with you in many of your ambitions. In fact, to coin a phrase, you might even say they're rooting for you.

Chance Encounters – and How to Make the Most of Them

No time like the present
Mary De La Riviere Manley, *The Lost Lover*

Chances are that by now you're getting heartily sick of all these discos and parties. Conceivably you can't even dance, or don't like loud music. While the latter can be solved by the use of boring old ear plugs it's not a trick which comes highly recommended. Your inability to dance does provide you with a far more entertaining and potentially productive opportunity. Learn. It is a well-known fact that of late many establishments designed to teach you all the tricks which made John Travolta successful have sprung up all over. Quite why anybody should wish to emulate an effeminate Italian person is unclear, but there it is. Or rather there they are. It is equally evident that in the main these places are full to bursting with a wide variety of nubile young ladies in various states of undress, and you could do no harm and perhaps great good by being in attendance yourself.

This will indubitably present you with a number of opportunities. At the same time it will also present you with a whole new set of problems. We have talked at some length of the opportunities available in discos and at parties or similar gatherings. While you may not be enormously enamoured of such venues they do, as we are agreed, have the saving grace of existing for the main purpose of allowing men and women to come together in an atmosphere of deep mental and sexual awareness for the implied purpose of ensuring that the human race avoids the fate which befell the unfortunate dinosaur.

Away from such places the situation is not so clear-cut. Sadly it is true that, no matter how often you attend musical emporia, you will meet more women outside their gilded halls than within them. These encounters will be on the bus, the train, in supermarkets, pubs, all sorts of places. They will be entirely accidental chance encounters without that degree of premeditation which so simplifies the pick-up process in discos.

If you meet a beautiful woman on the bus in the morning she is not mentally keyed up for your approaches. Indeed, she may not even be properly awake. This means that your task is somewhat harder, because it is now up to you to set the entire tone of the proceedings, and establish in her mind the atmosphere necessary to turn her mind to thoughts of romance. This, as you may imagine, is a tall order as the 9A thunders through the rush hour in the early hours of a cold winter morning. Nevertheless it is a problem which you are going to encounter repeatedly, and one which you will have to learn to solve if you are ever going to achieve the sort of regular success which you so earnestly seek.

To begin with you must be aware that such opportunities exist. If you ignore them you will never be able to realise their potential. So the first thing to remember is that your chances of getting to grips with an attractive example of the female of the species exists wherever you meet such a woman. And corny though it may sound it's worth repeating one word again; *wherever*. And if you think about that long enough you will at once realise that your opportunities are now boundless. We are no longer talking about deliberate hunting. We are no longer talking about selecting a venue and then selecting a suitable target. We are talking about the fact that the world is absolutely crammed with pretty girls; so crammed that you cannot possibly examine all the avenues open to you and still have time to work and sleep. There are, remember, only 24 hours in a day. All right, 25 if you skip lunch.

Given such a wide variety of choice you will see that all previous hints about spotting opportunities become doubly important if you are not to waste your time chasing up blind alleys or, worse still, chasing your own tail instead of somebody else's.

A long while ago, when I was still young and foolish instead of just foolish, I was fortunate enough to work with a man, Big Jim, whose company was not only agreeable but remarkably entertaining. Most of our business was conducted by telephone, and we had, during the course of a day, occasion to speak with a great number of young ladies. Sight unseen, they could have been Bardot or Medusa. We didn't know. But as a form of entertainment during the grind of the working day we adopted a game. House rules were that if you spoke to a woman on the phone then you were obliged to ask her out. Failure to comply with this regulation was punished; it was your round in the pub after work. Three failures meant three rounds before anybody else bought a drink. Faced with this sort of penalty it became quite easy to overcome any natural shyness you may have previously harboured, and you asked all women out without exception.

There are two things this teaches. First, you'd be stunned by the response. You'd be amazed at the number of women who agreed. We were. Second, you learned how to lead a conversation into this sort of area damn quick, otherwise you were permanently skint.

It's a worthwhile exercise for any man, this. Just try it yourself. You will, of course, need the co-operation of another man in your office, or you will need to be remarkably sure of your own self-discipline, because in order for an exercise of this nature to have any effect you will need the threat of some form of dreadful retribution, preferably financial, or else the spur to try is removed. But given the correct impetus it all works out. Whether or not you meet with any real degree of success in this is debatable. You will enjoy your working day a great deal more than was previously the case, however, and you will very swiftly learn how to capitalise on conversational opportunities or create such openings where none existed before.

It is hard at this point for anyone to give you any useful degree of practical advice on how to manipulate such conversations, since they are all, like people, unique. Consequently it is impossible to predict what openings will be offered to you. The best anyone can do is lay some ground rules to help you cope, as generally as possible, with whatever may crop up. Before we go into this let us remind ourselves that telephonic conversations of this sort, although they provide a degree of anonymity which encourages boldness, are not the only times at which you may wish to take advantage of a chance encounter. We must also look at the face-to-face kind, which are in all probability more frequent and which also, unhappily, offer greater potential for personal embarrassment.

Think back a moment; boldness and confidence play a major part in the attainment of success in discos and so on; at moments like this they are everything. Remember the old adage: nothing ventured, nothing gained. This remarkable piece of wisdom is expressed far more forcibly and appositely in the motto of that estimable branch of the armed services, the SAS: 'Who dares, wins'. True enough. But also remember that the SAS take a whole long time in training and preparation. Boldness alone is not sufficient.

Not to worry though, because you have read this far and are already much better prepared than was previously the case. You, we are both quite certain, have taken all precautions of cleanliness and so on in order to minimise the risk of failure. You are aware that you should constantly be on a war footing and are ready to enter into combat at any moment of the day. You are also very alert to situations at all times, because you know that you may be called upon to do battle anywhere at any time. In the street, on the bus, in the library, the pub, the office, any number of shops, even in the safety of your own home.

You are sufficiently perspicacious to realise that there are bound to be moments at which you will be forced to drop your guard. You know this is unavoidable and you are initially prepared to lose any chances which may arise at embarrassing moments. You may not actually have your pants round your ankles, but you know the moment at which a strategic withdrawal is vastly preferable to ignominious retreat following defeat by superior forces. Like all good soldiers you will put these moments aside, regarding them as being an unavoidable and useful experience.

Let us look now at those chance moments which arise when you are not so disadvantaged as to make anything but retreat inconceivable . . .

It doesn't matter about the location. We have mentioned a few possibilities but could never hope to cover all the options. All we can do is realise that the location, once it is outside the limits of traditionally-appointed mating grounds, is more or less immaterial. Your job now is to overcome such inhibiting barriers as are offered by the place and then make your move. It must be stressed that all previous rules apply. Check for obstacles like wedding rings and sturdily constructed boyfriends first. Now you must take steps to ascertain certain information. In discos or whatever the lady will be on the hunt also. It is reasonable to assume that on the neutral territory you are now confronted with she will not be as alert nor as mentally aware of the hunt as you are. Therefore she will not immediately begin to hand out all those signals of body-talk and so on which she would do in other situations possibly even without realising it. It is now up to you to do all the hard work.

There are two ways in which you may choose to go about this. You could, by blatant chat, inform her of your intentions and give her a chance to offer you that information in her usual subtle manner once she twigs exactly what you have in mind. Alternatively you could try to wheedle the necessary details out of her before she knows what's going on and has the chance to decide exactly what she wants you to know and what she doesn't.

In practice this latter is an extremely complicated ploy requiring great verbal dexterity on the part of the operator. It has the added penalty of arousing suspicion and creating a defensive barrier if it is detected before it has had a chance to run its course, and should therefore only be undertaken if you are dead certain that you are smart enough and glib enough to get away with it or if you are only passingly interested in the outcome and wouldn't really mind losing out on this particular opportunity. Nine times out of 10 the degree of sly deceitful treachery needed to bring this to a successful conclusion eliminates it from the repertoire of most men (who are nice people) and marks it out as being the exclusive preserve of highly-skilled lounge-lizards who won't need any help from me. Which means that we must consider only the first tactic.

This conveniently brings us back to the business of turning a conversation round to a point at which the lady in question has no doubt as to your intentions and has sufficient opportunity to make her signals. The benefits of this are twofold. It either saves you making a complete arse of yourself in a no-go situation or has the exact opposite effect, allowing you to proceed secure in the knowledge that you're doing all right so far and that everybody knows precisely what it is you're doing.

So how do you bring about this idyllic arrangement? The first thing is to remove the conversation as far away as possible from whatever subject was its initial basis. That is because in these engagements we assume that you and this lady have been brought together in order to deal with one of the trivia of modern life. She works at the Gas Board and is taking the money for your bill, or is working out what fine you have to pay for keeping three Biggles books out of the library for a year as opposed to the customary two weeks. We assume that it is a business transaction of some sort, then.

It is exceptionally difficult to move from discussing the number of therms your water heater consumes per hour to an animated conversation about whether or not she likes Mahler and would appreciate hearing some on the exceptionally fine stereo you've bought as a result of withholding payment on the gas bill. We will deal with this shortly. Meanwhile let's continue to manipulate the present conversation. This is startlingly simple to achieve. All it requires is a basic understanding of human nature; all human nature, not just the female kind.

My Mum used to say to me 'Flattery will get you nowhere'. I expect your Mum said it to you too. The fascinating thing about that is that my Dad never said it once, and I bet yours didn't either. It's almost exclusively a feminine preserve, and there's a very good reason why this should be so. It's because that simple, but impressive-sounding statement is a fat lie. Flattery, my friend, will get you practically anywhere.

Flattery may take a variety of forms but in the end it works because it relies on one basic principle. Take anybody you like as an example, male or female, married or single, young or old, and ask yourself: what is this person's favourite topic of conversation? What are they most happy to talk about? In every case the answer's the same. People like talking about themselves more than anything else in the world. They enjoy being told that they are rich, clever, talented, better than you, good-looking, witty, charming or any damn thing as long as it's complimentary. And while women are clever people who are very hard to deceive it is on this subject they are most vulnerable and it is when discussing themselves that they are most likely to believe practically anything they are told. This is because women, like all human beings, believe what they want to believe more readily than anything else. Oh yes, flattery is the most powerful weapon in your armoury at this point.

Since women are not silly most of them are already aware of this particular truism, and are consequently always on their guard lest they fall for it. This being so you will immediately realise that it is a tool you must employ most carefully. Being obvious is out of the question, and you must learn to adopt the more subtle forms of approach.

There is without any doubt a certain advantage available should you approach a strange woman and simply say 'You are the most beautiful woman I have ever seen in my life.' However she is bound to treat this statement with a high degree of suspicion, and no wonder. Bear in mind also that this is an approach which will only ever stand a chance with a stranger. It's no good saying it to someone you've known for a while just because you're alone one evening. She will ask herself how come you never mentioned it before, and a brief examination of your circumstances will lead her directly to the correct answer, viz, ie and namely you're lying through your teeth and are simply after a swift portion of ferocity. While this may not preclude her accepting your advances it definitely lowers the odds. Honesty is something we must examine separately at a later date.

It is much more subtle to ask her a question. Apart from being subtle it does also mean that she has to answer you, which is after all the entrée into conversation you're looking for. Therefore you may do better with something like 'What's it like being the most beautiful woman in the room/bus/building/world?' You've given her your opinion, flattered her tremendously and ever so politely. She now may answer you without commitment on either side, although she is immediately aware of your interest in her. The answer you get will tell you how to proceed, or whether you should go and perform the physical impossibility she has just suggested.

This is the sort of approach you should adopt with women when you have no legitimate call to enter into conversation with them, like your gas bill. Alternatives are also available. Tell her she has beautiful eyes, lovely hair, or that she is exceptionally well-dressed. Women like compliments about things like this; their physical appearance is very important to them, especially their clothing, and you cannot possibly blot your copybook or anything else by being nice about such things. Her grateful acceptance of your compliment won't necessarily stop her thinking that you're the ugliest little bastard she's ever seen in her life, but that's the way the breaks go.

Things like this can be good fun; if you always treat them as such, and don't expect to get your rocks off on the spot you will enjoy life much more than you did before and will probably be agreeably surprised by the results. Remember you're playing percentages, and remember that nothing puts women off more than desperation. It implies failure, and no-one loves a failure.

With this in the back of your mind you will probably realise that this sort of meeting is the moment at which you should attempt to employ a little humour. It is far more appropriate than in a dance-hall, without in any way reducing the effect or clarity of your intentions. 'You are the sort of girl I could fall madly in lust with' is relatively amusing but retains a singleness of purpose which should be unmistakeable. At the same time it won't earn you any black eyes as long as you don't back it up with a swift grope or a pinch on the bum.

I've heard a lot of men pull the old 'Will you marry me?' ploy on total strangers in the past. This is a quite acceptable entrée provided it is delivered with the right degree of levity. It has the added advantage of having only two possible answers – yes or no. If the answer's 'yes' you've just connected, while if it's 'no' you can still continue the line with something like 'Perhaps you're right – How about we just live together for a while?' The important thing is not to lose the thread, from which it is clear that almost any question is better than a statement, since it requires an answer; while a question which has the minimum possible number of responses not only clarifies the position but also allows you to have a ready store of supplementary questions or remarks with which to prolong the exchange.

There are an infinite number of tricks like this. Asking directions in the street is one. But don't waste the opportunity. You could quite easily go up to a pretty girl in the street and ask for directions to somewhere you already know, or a street you've just invented and hope to spark off a conversation from there. Who knows, you may well achieve excellent results. But you'd do far better to be more positive about it. After all, whether she knows the way or not the chances are she'll answer you and shove off fairly quickly. This is because she's not expecting a pick-up routine in Regent Street or wherever, and unless you're an expert with body talk or have just poured a pint of Dettol in your eyes she's never going to know what you had in mind, is she?

No, she's not.

So ask her the way to a pub or restaurant you know about. That way, if she says, yes, she knows where it is, or, no she doesn't, you're in with another line. If yes you say 'Isn't it nice, would you like a drink?' and if no you say 'Really, it's ever so nice there, why don't I buy you a drink?'

Or ask her the time. Whether she knows or not you're still in with something like 'Well, I always have a little bottle of champagne about now, would you care to join me?'

The only rule is – think positive. Don't allow the moment to pass without giving yourself the opportunity to slide a polite invitation into the conversation in a natural way. No-one will be offended by it, and nor will you be upset, annoyed or embarrassed if it's turned down. You'd be surprised by the number of women who are genuinely pleased by this sort of flattery. The very least you'll get is a smile, maybe lots more. But you won't know if you don't try. And neither will she. Why deprive a beautiful woman of the pleasure of your company and a chance to get to know you and love you?

By now you'll definitely have got the idea and won't need further help in these moments. Beyond doubt you'll work out your own lines in advance and soon learn how to either engineer them or make them up as you go along. Just as long as you know that the world is full of opportunity asking to be grabbed, although you shouldn't take that too literally unless you wish to get arrested with alarming frequency.

You will notice that in the course of all this we still haven't moved very far away from the field of flattery, albeit less than overt. The simple act of inviting a lady to drink with you is a kind of flattery, never mind all that stuff about her being more beautiful than a spring sunrise which you've doubtless been rambling on about when you thought I wasn't listening. It's surprising how many men mistake slush for cool compliment, and even more of a shock to discover how many men are actually sloppy and sentimental themselves. Gentlemen, there is a time and place for everything and Neasden High Road isn't the place, whatever the time is.

But flattery is what we're dealing with, so let's continue. We've covered the area of personal compliment, both direct and implied, but it is still possible to imply a great deal more without being caught in the act with the syrup-tin raised to our lips.

We know that people like talking about themselves, and women especially enjoy preening themselves in the glow of such reflected praise, even if they do owe it all to Max Factor and Vidal Sassoon. There are still further avenues open to you though, you silver-tongued rascal, as long as you realise it.

Like any human, women enjoy praise; they like talking about themselves. If you could combine these two areas of interest you would surely be onto a winning formula, would you not? Course you would, course you would. And what's the easiest way to go about this? Bearing in mind we're talking about the lady in the library, or perhaps the lady taking your money at the Gas Board. Obvious, isn't it? Talk about her work. It is, after all, a subject of great moment in her life. And it gives you a chance to admire her manifold achievements while giving her a chance to expound on them at considerable length without boasting. And all the time you're talking about something which is very close to her heart; you'd have to look a long way to get odds like that in conversation about anything else.

The most important thing is for you to ask a few relevant questions and let her answer them at as much length as she wishes. Although the odd admiring murmur won't be out of place you should avoid fulsome praise; this will eventually arouse her suspicions and alert her to your true (and utterly nefarious) intentions. The hardest thing in the world is to listen to someone else extolling their own virtues, but you must master the art; good listeners are hard to find and are much appreciated by all and sundry. This is one certain way of making yourself startlingly popular in any company, never mind just that of women you hope to know better, not to mention carnally, ASAP.

You will find, when speaking to this lady, that very few people appreciate her real worth, or have a true understanding of the kind of hardships with which she is forced to cope on every day of her working life. She will be deeply gratified by your warm and sympathetic nature, impressed by your immediate grasp of the overall situation (your silence, which obviates the possibility of verbal blunders, will ensure that she will believe this last impossibility to be true) and, of course, hugely flattered by your interest and concern. Your quiet, almost inaudible suggestion that you discuss it in greater depth this evening should meet with unqualified success as long as it is sufficiently underplayed and correctly timed. This kind of interest in her mind rather than her physical attributes is especially useful when dealing with intelligent women of a liberated disposition, who are just as much women as all the others, and therefore just as susceptible to this kind of subtle flattery, if not more so.

It is also worthwhile noting that this kind of thing doesn't only apply to ladies in libraries and Gas Boards. It is a valuable second line of approach, when used as a follow-up, with any woman whose acquaintance you have just made whether it be on the bus, in the street or the queue for the supermarket checkout. Get her talking, then get her to talk about herself – either her job or her personal interests.

If she works in a shop of some sort then even if you know exactly what you want, whether it be food, clothes, hi-fi or books, ask her advice. It is yet another fascinating and exceptionally useful human trait that everybody likes to appear clever. If by being ignorant, or feigning ignorance, you can engender this kind of superiority in her mind you will yet again be on to a winning streak. Women do like their men to be men, but they still like to feel good at something, and if that something is their profession then so much the better. Also, everybody, but everybody, hates a smartarse know-all.

This is something worthy of further consideration. Asking a woman to help you with something, even if you are perfectly convinced that you could manage it unaided, is no stupid thing. Cut your hand? Don't make a fuss or start wingeing, but do get her to put a plaster on it. Brings out her maternal instincts if not a feeling of superiority. Even pretending to be horrified by the sight of your own blood isn't that daft, as long as you only do so in the face of insignificant little scratches. Remember to be stoically indifferent to severed limbs and arteries, especially if they're your own.

The rule here is not to overdo it and always employ a proper sense of occasion. She won't relish the prospect of her man demonstrating a yellow streak a mile wide in company; rather she'll be a bit dischuffed. But she won't mind in privacy, when there's just the two of you. Indeed, on those occasions when it happens in public she'll recall your private agonies and be even more impressed by your bravery.

Everybody likes a fool about the place. It makes them feel that much better by comparison. Just don't be too big a fool is all.

You may think that we've exhausted the possibilities contained within the practise of the ignoble art of flattery, in which case you'd be wrong. You may also think we've used up all the possibilities of coincidental meetings, and you'd be wrong about that too. It is not for me to make a list of all the places where you may possibly meet a woman who might be susceptible to your fatal charm and your irresistible line in smoothtalk, mostly because I don't know all the places you go. Wherever they are it is there where you should look for the opportunities; swimming pool, ice rink, horse races, Twickenham, local Watneys emporium, all of them.

We may not do ourselves any harm to think about your hobbies, if you've got any which actually bear scrutiny, that is. Hobbies, you see, tend to fall into three broad categories. The first is the kind which gives you warts in the palm of your hand and occasions frequent visits to the optician to have your prescription boosted. It is hardly my place to admonish you for the disgusting nature of your personal habits, so I won't. The other two kinds of hobby are totally acceptable in polite society and may be reasonably successfully described as either being of a social nature or of an introspective and solitary kind. An example of the social kind would perhaps be cricket, and the second, let's say, stamp collecting.

It doesn't matter what they are, or which category they fall into. Yet. Whatever the case it is reasonable to assume that you are enthusiastic about them (or it), yes? Naturally you are sensible enough not to try to convert everybody you meet, but you will still be pleased to prattle endlessly to the first person you meet who demonstrates a more than polite interest or who, even more excitingly, *shares* your interest.

Women have hobbies and interests as well. If you meet a woman in the Tate Gallery it would be remarkably shrewd of you to use art in general, and preferably the bit of it she happens to be looking at, as your opening gambit rather than 'See Chelsea lost again on Saturday'. This is clearly not a point which needs to be laboured since you will have made this sort of elementary deduction yourself, Watson. You might care to consider three aspects of the overall view, however.

Firstly you should try to engage the lady in conversation and then let her do the talking. Flatter her by being interested in her subject, flatter her by listening to what she has to say. If she leaves you for dead and about two days' sailing beyond the three mile limit, never mind out of your depth, you have two choices. Tell her she's a damn sight more knowledgeable on this than you are and then try to adopt the mien of a diligent but intelligent pupil or shut up and wait for her to finish. Don't pretend to be smart if you're not, because she'll cross you off the list so fast you'll think Concorde goes everywhere in reverse, and do not, under any circumstances try to change the subject either politely or by brute force, because she will think, probably quite rightly, that you are an ignorant bleeder not worth the time of day, with fewer manners than the average earthworm.

If it becomes immediately clear that you are a great deal better informed on the subject than she is you still only have one choice if you don't wish to behave like an arrogant and insensitive pig; listen to her point of view. If you are obliged to correct her knowledge then do so quietly and politely. If the opinions she expresses appear to be based on incorrect or insufficient information then do not ridicule her unless you know how to do so humorously and without causing offence. Do so as unobtrusively as you possibly can. In other words flatter her by not simply writing off her knowledge (or lack of it) as being worthy of scorn, but rather as something which deserves your entire consideration before you finally decide what your opinion is likely to be. In many circles this practice is regarded as an elementary courtesy accorded to even the most dim-witted, but you'd be very surprised by the number of men who forget about it when faced with a woman over whom they wish to demonstrate their male superiority – presumably in the hopeless belief that a deep knowledge of Impressionist painters also implies vast sexual attraction and ability.

In a great many cases and situations people will always listen to a talker who is an expert in his field. If you are such an expert then there is no problem. There are, however, few things possessed of a boredom more terminal than the egocentric ramblings of someone who is ignorant enough to believe himself an expert when he isn't. It is a trap well worth avoiding.

These three difficulties are less likely to arise if your hobby falls into the 'social' classification. That is, one which requires the involvement and participation of yourself and/or others. We have cited cricket as an example of this, which is perhaps a trifle misleading, since this is a game which requires the participation of 22 people, not many of whom are likely to be women, who are then surrounded by a great number of other, uninvolved types (who are generally speaking asleep most of the time). Being a spectator of an active sport or hobby puts you at exactly the same risk as being a practitioner of a solitary hobby; all such spectators may refer again to all the remarks above, while genuine participants may continue.

'Doing' hobbies provide you with several advantages. One of these is of course the fact that, since they generally involve physical jerks of some kind, they tend to involve long periods of recuperation in licensed hostelries afterwards, thus providing an ideal breeding ground, so to speak, for romance.

Further, as those of you already involved will doubtless be aware, they also involve the participation of scantily-clad ladies, and the prurient pleasures this affords should most definitely not be overlooked. If you do not already belong to a club concerned with badminton, tennis or squash or some such then your attentions are commended to the possibilities attendant upon this sort of thing.

The biggest face-saver available from active hobbies is that varying degrees of skill are at once apparent; if you are a superb player then you will be able to do all your boasting, amply demonstrating your prowess, on court or wherever. Likewise if the lady is better at it than you then you will know in advance, and will not be tempted to cock it all up by pretending to be Jonah Barrington when you're really Frank Spencer. You have the added bonus of being able to ask for, or offer, coaching in your chosen field, preferably in private. The possibilities here need hardly be spelled out for you.

This does not mean that the non-active hobbyists among us need be unduly worried. Many a fair lady has succumbed to an invitation to 'come up and see my stamp collection', a ploy which may be valuable even if you don't have one, as long as you can later deliver the 'actually I lied about that, I just wanted to be alone with you' line with sufficient panache and sincerity.

Even if you don't have a hobby you're not without opportunities, then. A slurred invitation to 'Come up and see my retchings' has been known to work, as have other even more implausible suggestions. If I tell you that 'I've got these two ringside tickets for the South-Eastern Mouse Olympics, taking place in my bedroom later this evening' has actually met with success on one occasion then the non-hobbyists among you will doubtless take heart.

What we must be striving for, at all times, is to be polite, not pushy or overbearing, but still make our intentions reasonably plain. Remember, we are dealing here with a lady who, in all probability, we will never see again, so there's no time for messing about. You have nothing to lose and everything to gain from giving it a try. You'll kick yourself for weeks if you allow something wonderful to slip through your fingers without making at least a little bit of effort, and so will she, in all probability. And it doesn't take much effort, at least initially. You'll only have to work at it once you seem to be making headway, and you can quite happily write it all off as a pleasant interlude if you're making none.

Ladies you already know, or who you are guaranteed to see again, are an entirely different subject and need to be treated completely differently. It is in long-term situations that you will have to try hardest, but it is also in these situations that you can let your imagination run riot and give yourself up to the pleasures of the chase. Who knows, you might even catch something....

Long-Term Strategy

You made me love you
I didn't want to do it
Joseph McCarthy, *You made me love you*

Doubtless you've seen the chocolate ads on the box where the mysterious ice-cream in the natty black gear leaps tall buildings in a single bound and does a lot of late-night stunting and swimming simply in order to deliver a box of sweeties to some simpering tart, possibly on the occasion of her birthday. Quite conceivably you may believe that all he's proved by this wimpish ploy is that he is a prize wally with nothing better to do and insufficient imagination or courage to approach the lady in question directly to plight his troth with a view to removing her undergarments at mach 7. Under the circumstances it is hardly surprising that you should feel this way, but before you dismiss the episode as being one of the more crass examples of the commercial-makers' art perhaps you should consider its wider implications.

A great number of commercials use a similar techique, employing the lure of beautiful women in order to sell a given product. Of late it has become popular to decry this sort of thing as being 'sexploitation' and degrading to women. While the sexploitation angle is completely undeniable it is hard to avoid the feeling that all these liberationist types have screwed up on the rest of it, and got it all back to front. Certainly the presence of quantities of scantily-clad women in adverts of all kinds is irrefutable, but it is becoming increasingly more difficult to regard them as being the victims; it is rather the poor unfortunate male, whose desire for the persons of nubile nymphets is entirely natural, who is being wrung through an emotional mangle of giant proportions.

The promise is evident in all of this kind of thing. Drive this type of car, smoke this kind of tobacco or cigarette, wear these clothes, drive a lorry and eat vast quantities of chocolate; those are the messages. But all advertising has to offer some form of inducement. 'Buy this and save a fortune'; 'drink this beer and watch your willy grow to giant proportions'. The trick is to convince people that if they do one thing you want them to do then something they want very badly will automatically happen PDQ.

All too often the natural and healthy reproductive urges of the male population are being exploited in this way. Eat a certain type of margarine or wear a silly hat and smoke this kind of aromatic pipe tobacco and millions of ravishingly attractive women will swoon at your feet; they'll queue up in the street simply in the hope of being able to touch the hem of your (very expensive) hand-made suiting as you sweep past on the way to your personal heliport. In fact it would seem that if you followed the dictates of our noble advertising agencies you would become a millionaire overnight and do for women what the Pied Piper did for rats and children.

However ridiculous this may at first appear, try watching the box for a few hours and actually looking at the ads instead of nipping out for a wee. You'll find it becomes increasingly more difficult to avoid the belief that scrubbing your armpits with certain proprietary brands of wire-wool scouring pads will make you sexually attractive to frustrated housewives the length and breadth of Milton Keynes.

Despite the evidently risible nature of such suppositions there is, regrettably, a more than passing amount of truth in a number of these garish blandishments. This applies less to the use of disinfectant than to the provision of chocolates and the like. The fairy with the box of Crunchy Frog Surprise Sugar-Coated Bon-Bons is onto a fairly good thing. He is also making use of a time-honoured ruse which, mostly by virtue of its age, has fallen from common usage. We must not neglect it, since it can be particularly effective in our chosen field.

Now, although approaching strange women in libraries, art galleries, museums and even pet shops can produce a substantial degree of success and may conceivably gain you entry to the Kingdom of Heaven (although not the Guinness Book of Records unless you are especially proficient or lucky) it is not by any means the only way to achieve happiness and peace of mind. Nor is it even remotely the most enjoyable way of employing your time and talents in the quest for untold pleasures of the flesh.

The age of chivalry is quite possibly dead. Some may go so far as to say it is positively decomposed. But chivalry wasn't only the nonsense about holding doors open and giving up your seat on the train to pretty girls. Along with chivalry something far more entertaining and important passed on to join the *houris* of paradise. It was the ancient but not very noble art of seduction. The modern film industry would have you believe that seduction is a process whereby you rip the clothes forcibly from every woman you meet prior to indulging in a degree of strenuous calisthenics which would make Johnny Weismuller quail in fearful anticipation. This is a rather misleading point of view which needs to be corrected at once if you're ever going to have any fun out of it.

At this point fun and straightforward results tend to diverge somewhat. The blunt street pick-up routines, if performed in sufficient quantity, will always meet with more success than a prolonged seduction. They aren't half as pleasurable though, and seduction, if carried out properly, will always meet with a higher percentage level of success. Since it takes a great deal longer you will see that seducers eventually carve fewer notches on their bedposts (or wherever they choose to carve them) than the more direct among us. But, as we've said, seducers have more fun and are often much nicer people than you think they are. They tend to get more pleasure from every liaison simply because they put more into it and it is for the individual to decide which category suits him best. It seems quite possible to be both; there is no reason why you should not conduct a long-term seduction alongside any number of quick sallies (or sheilas) and thus enjoy the very best of both worlds.

Successful seduction depends upon entirely different principles to those employed by the day-trippers and requires different attitudes. The first thing to remember here is that it is not necessary to bung all your cards on the table within two minutes. In fact it is generally a lot better if you make a point of not doing so. You have got, after all, plenty of time on your hands and can thus afford to play them slowly. It is not even mandatory for you to win each engagement; all you have to do is come out of it with sufficient tricks to take the rubber. Be prepared to lose a few of these skirmishes and content yourself with simply winning the battle. This ambition will be much aided by the fact that you know there is a battle under way which stretches further into the future than the lady under siege will believe. In this way you will always be able to remain one step ahead of the game.

The technique of seduction may be usefully employed in two different modes; either when faced with a recalcitrant lady who has rejected your initial advances or when faced with a lady you believe will only respond to this kind of approach but who is, as yet, unaware of your strictly dishonourable intentions. Its practice also serves useful purposes at one or two other junctures, but these we shall deal with in the fullness of time. For the present let's concentrate just on these two.

Luckily for both of us it makes little difference which of the two situations you are confronted with; the tactics remain the same. It is still worth pointing out that ladies ignorant of your desires are far more susceptible to this technique than the forewarned kind, and it is possible for you to utilise, at least initially, a number of insidious methods of winning her favour.

Briefly summarised, all this involves is becoming her friend and winning such amounts of her trust as she is willing to place in your wholly unworthy (and doubtless sweaty) palms. Bear in mind that since time is of no significance whatever you can devote as many weeks or months to this as you feel suitable. There is a more than a fair chance that if she is even faintly aware of the sort of machinations to which men are prone she will read your mind and correctly deduce your intentions almost immediately; probably the first time you buy her a drink, give her a lift home or send her a card on her birthday. However your strange reluctance to follow this up with an invitation to dinner in some shady locale within a few hours will either lull her at once into that happy state known as a sense of false security or convince her you are playing hard to get. It doesn't matter which of these alternatives occur, since the effect will be almost exactly the same. In practice, now that liberated times are upon us, the 'hard to get' syndrome may arouse her own fighting instincts and she may actually attempt to lure you into her own trap, probably out of pique. Your choices then are to either capitalise at once or ignore it all completely, leaving her in splendid isolation. The first course is the easier of the two. Indeed the second may often be almost impossible, depending upon how alluring she is. Do try only to give in to her advances if you are certain she is not simply trying to assert her attractiveness over an ignorant male and will take you for a short but unproductive ride to the nearest expensive restaurant.

Assuming that all goes according to plan (yours, not hers) you will then be ready to embark upon your seduction proper. It is most important that you realise before you commence the nature of your task. Timing is absolutely vital in all of this and it is essential that you get it right lest you place the success of the whole operation in jeopardy. Seduction may only be properly conducted at one of two speeds; very slowly and gentlemanly or at full bore. Mixing the two will lead to disaster. The slow kind is conducted at a mild, but accelerating pace, a curve of a parabolic nature gradually rising to a gentle crescendo. This does not involve breaking into an unseemly run towards its closing stages but merely indicates a polite build-up. It is again vital that you should not confuse this increase in pressure and effort with the frenetic attack of the 'head-over-heels' (with any luck) faster method.

All of this will become clear. Let us first regard the swifter of the two. As opposed to the gradual siege nature of the polite variety this relies upon a technique of constant and overwhelming bombardment over a period preferably of days but possibly one or two weeks. It should not be maintained for any longer than this, partly because it puts reasonable strain on the operator and partly because it entails considerable financial outlay over a very short period of time. Your bank manager will advise you that the time has come to desist if you fail to heed any other advice, and this is a situation to be avoided at all, er, costs.

There are, you see, a variety of weapons in the seducer's armoury, but many of them will have to be purchased from various establishments who depend for their commercial viability upon the continuing nature of male carnal gluttony. A few – a very few – cost little if nothing, but these are weapons to be employed only by experts, as they require a high degree of skill in order to obtain maximum effect, and mishandled can quite easily lead the whole endeavour into disaster.

Let us assume, then, that you have selected a lady on whose person you would like to exercise your not inconsiderable physical talents. Let us further assume that, for reasons of your own, you have decided to adopt the Blitzkrieg Technique. In this, as in any other campaign, you will be much aided by the nature of women, all of whom believe that they are Venus personified as any man would doubtless realise at once, had he but the good sense to stop ogling the obvious and transitory talents of Hot Gossip and delve beneath her acne and generosity of waistline to the real, sensuous woman lurking beneath. It is at once clear that your slimy, underhanded attempts at seduction will only serve to confirm what she has always believed and consequently she will have won half the battle (the psychological half) for you the minute you open hostilities. This you will do in short order.

First, try and think about her; is she romantic, practical, cerebral, what? While all women are indubitably romantics to some degree many of them submerge this aspect beneath their interest in the plays of William Congreve or the films of some obscure Czechoslovakian director whose name you can't even spell, never mind pronounce. If this is the case (and you are urged to find out soonest) then remember it for a later date, for this will be your trump card. First it is your obligation and your duty to let her know that you, as a deeply understanding and intelligent male, have spotted the salient fact which others have missed. Namely that she is a desperately beautiful and attractive woman dying to be released from her shell and grow to a true awakening of her full potential, mostly as a result of your tender ministrations. This effect may be achieved in a variety of ways. You could wait for her birthday, Christmas or Valentine's day, but such overtures are open to an amount of misinterpretation and may be construed simply as politeness. Better to start today, since Blitzkrieg is what you have in mind.

As a general rule the opening of such a campaign is best conducted without a proper declaration of war; that is to say your first overtures should, while not actually being anonymous (don't want some other bugger getting all the credit, do we?) preferably be conducted through some third party or other, like Interflora.

This is where we come back to the pansy with the chocolates and the never-ending supply of black polo-neck jumpers. He is not silly, but simply pandering to his sweetheart's whim of being spoilt. Women like to be spoilt. For the Blitzkrieg to work you've got to spoil her like she's never been spoilt before. In this kind of situation as every woman knows, big is most decidedly beautiful, whatever the agony columnists would have you believe. It is quite in order to send her presents. Lots of them. One is about as much use to you now as a hairbrush to Yul Brynner.

Sending a lady flowers is something which has fallen far out of favour in recent times. Even if the lady in question professes to hate the men who send her flowers more than she hates the plants themselves I can tell you that unless she suffers from prodigious bouts of hay fever she is a liar. Send her some. Better still, send her loads. The repetition trick will come in handy here. Remember you've got to do this sort of thing to excess; a bunch of flowers is no good at all. It has recently been considered romantic to send women a single rose in a box. This form of gentle understatement is all very well in its place but has no part in your present tactics. Nothing less than a dozen roses will suffice. Two dozen are twice as good. In order to go completely over the top it is even better to send her twelve red jobs every day for a week. If nothing else happens, sooner or later she'll run out of vases and be forced to ring you up just to ask you stop. It is at this point you may satisfactorily negotiate a deal along the lines of 'I'll stop sending the flowers if . . .'

Sending flowers alone (with, of course, a suitably obscure message card) is not enough, even if you have gone to the dozen a day extreme. It is no earthly use sitting back on your laurels waiting for some sort of result. You must follow up any advantage you may already have gained as swiftly as possible and in any case within 48 hours. You will find, especially during the slack months of the year away from Christmas or Easter, etc, that card shops are packed to overflowing with an astounding variety of missives designed to convey all manner of sentiments, both seemly and unseemly. Whatever else you do, it is imperative that you do not make the mistake of buying just one of these. Buy yourself a handful and despatch them at minimum intervals of 24 hours. Try to grade both the printed message within the card and any inscriptions which you choose to add so that the import of each successive arrival is stronger and more transparent than its immediate forerunner. From this it will at once be clear that you should sit down and write them all together, sending them off one by one in the correct order.

The last of these cards should be designed to arrive on about the fifth day of anonymous floral tributes. By this time the lady should be in no doubts as to the identity and intention of the provider of all this, although you still may not be in direct contact with her.

The last two days of flower arrival should be liberally sprinkled with telemessages. These things are vastly expensive, which is why you save them to the end, in the hope that long before now she will have cracked and got breathlessly and enthusiastically in touch with you. It will cost you about two quid just to put the address on a telegram, so you are advised to keep the messages as brief as possible. Once again these epigrams (if such they be) should be in ascending order of relevance, and should all be composed prior to the sending of the first one. Sadly the telegram service sends off everything the minute it arrives, so unless you want them to arrive in a disorderly clutch you are advised to visit the post office at regular, but well-spaced intervals – two or three the first day (the sixth since you first opened your campaign) and perhaps more on the final day.

As a rule the Post Office include the time of despatch along with the address at the top of a telegram, so Madam can hardly fail to be impressed by your persistence and your devotion.

Unless she considers you to be a pathetic weed of less significance than the ice in her dry Martini, in which case you are pursuing a lost cause and should have had the good sense to realise it long before you spent all this money, the time is now ripe for you to strike your final blow, and this must be done in person. Get on the dog and bone about halfway through the final day of attack and invite her somewhere she can't resist. It is at this juncture that your previous research into her personal preferences for obscure European films, etc will pay dividends. If she has no such pronounced taste then you should take her somewhere splendid, for which read expensive. She will always say that money doesn't impress her, and she always likes men for what they are rather than what they've got, but while this may be essentially true it will not preclude her being mightily pleased by your desire to expend sums larger than the National Debt in pursuit of her favours.

It is quite possible that her preferences for things esoteric may lead to a situation whereby you cannot escort her to the place of her dreams for some time. For example the next offering by the Sadler's Wells bunch may not be for some weeks; her favourite band may not be in concert for a few months, even. Do not despair. If you are unable to offer a near approximation (many pop bands substitute reasonably for each other, and almost any example of live theatre will stand in for another) then acquire tickets for this far-off event and invite her to attend same in your company. Once she has accepted (and let's face it, while she may have previous engagements for tonight no woman can predict with any credibility that she will be washing her hair on one particular evening seven weeks hence) then is your moment to express pleasure at her acceptance but suggest that since it is so far off perhaps she would care to become involved with something less earth-shattering (like going almost anywhere) in the more immediate future – how about tonight?

Now, while women will appreciate, and even expect, the bold approach, requiring that you invite them out this very evening, no messing, it is quite possible that she will be otherwise engaged. Notwithstanding this you should make the offer for tonight. Expect to get turned down, but expect to lose many points if you don't ask.

Before we go on to the next step in the Blitzkrieg let us go back to the slow approach once more, since from this point on the two strategies tend to merge somewhat.

The polite method requires that you begin operations at a suitably opportune moment rather than right out of the blue. Commence on her birthday or some suitable national feast-day with the appropriate card and, should the occasion demand, some small, but immaculately conceived gift. Cards are one thing. They open proceedings, set the stage for the next move and are sufficiently bland as to be open to a number of interpretations. Your ideal here is to create in the lady the belief that you *may* be pursuing her, but also leave room for enough doubt to get her own innate curiosity (women are worse than all feline species put together in this) aroused. A suitably oblique card, then, with a suitably ambiguous message, is what you're looking for. This much is relatively easy. Choosing gifts is no such thing.

A box of sweeties is a cop-out and will correctly be regarded as such. A bunch of flowers is quite nice, but also a bit of a cop-out at this moment. A single rose, unannounced, on a birthday or similar, is weedy, although a rose a day for two or three days is obvious but nice. An orchid is neither. Orchids do not suffer from the connotations attached to roses by the female brain. While any of these things will suffice should no better alternative present itself you should be at a stage when you can do much better than this by now.

But caution is now of the essence. You all know the joke about women choosing their apparel, but like so many other jokes on the subject of romance it isn't that funny since it is largely born from a considerable amount of truth.

I swear that this happened to me once. We were going out for the evening. Nowhere that special, simply a very nice Italian restaurant we were wont to frequent. Madam didn't wear dresses very often, but had decided that tonight was to be an exception. A great deal of deep consideration eventually produced a short list of two. She sought my advice and with some foreboding I prepared to give it. Basically it was a 'This one or this one?' choice. I chose one. She said not a word but simply assumed that martyred expression of one who has been hard-hit by the slings and arrows of outrageous fortune but is too polite and too brave to mention it. 'I suppose,' quoth I, though I should have known better, 'that you're wondering what's wrong with the other one?' To my great surprise and even greater consternation the answer was 'Yes'. She wasn't joking.

This is always a danger with women. Buy her a new coat and she bursts into tears because you obviously didn't like the one she's been wearing all this time. Buy her, insignificantly, a bottle of perfume and she cracks up because you clearly didn't like the way she smelt previously. Doubtless you have a clear grasp of the overall picture by now, and are aware that the purchase of gifts for ladies is an operation fraught with pitfalls. Nevertheless it is a minefield into which you are going to be forced to venture and quite soon.

Wait for the right moment. If you've just sent her a card for any of the possible reasons we have talked of – allow a decent interval to elapse. Then present her with a small token of your esteem. Flowers cannot offend and can successfully be ascribed to it being a beautiful day and you felt like doing something foolish for someone beautiful or even to celebrate some personal achievement of your own. 'I've just cleared off my overdraft and I bought you these to celebrate.'

Anything of a more personal nature will require a bit more tact, since the possiblity of a perceived insult is so real. Perfume is safer than clothing (bet you don't know her size anyway) since it is quite possible that your tastes in female fashion may not coincide. Anyway it's easier to brush off an unlucky choice with scents, since some of them (especially the oil-based perfume as opposed to Eau de Toilettes) smell wonderful on one person but are reminiscent of sewage on another. With clothing you are generally obliged to take the lady with you on a shopping expedition. This is not out of the question, but be careful. Especially in the sort of shop which is not in the habit of pricing its merchandise she will infallibly pick out the most expensive item, usually at twenty paces. This is something which is perhaps better reserved for later in the offensive.

Start with flowers and then move on to perfume. Just give it to her and say it's a beautiful scent, so feminine, that you felt sure it would be truly stunning dabbed behind her ears as opposed to anybody else's. There are a number of general-purpose scents which fulfil this role, all of them expensive. Avoid the common things, like *Rive Gauche* or whatever, and aim for something really feminine. *Chanel No 5* fits this bill but suffers from being something of a cliché in its field. While the cliché is still the quickest form of communication known to man it is something we are presently trying to avoid. *Femme* by Rochas is better, as would be Worth's *Je Reviens* or Guerlain's *Ode*.

This compliment to her femininity will never go amiss and should again be delivered well after your last overture of flowers. By now, over a period of weeks, you will have sent her a card, bought some flowers and followed up with perfume. Gradually she is getting the message. Also she will begin to realise that you are a man of much greater depth than she had at first perceived. All those things that everybody says about you (his whole body's nothing more than a giant periscope for his willy, and so on) will demonstrably be the envious and scurrilous prattlings of those who are dim enough not to have seen through your cynical shell and beyond to the real, sensitive you. So far, so good.

Your next task will be twofold. You must confirm this belief in her mind and also convince her that she is the person who brings out this very sensitivity, while all the philistines around her have failed. This seemingly impossible task is a pushover. Take her out; anywhere will do, theatre, cinema, dinner, business function. Take her because you've been let down by someone else, or hate going on your own. She won't believe you, but by now she'll be more than ready to go with you secure in the knowledge that it is merely your natural reticence which forces you to adopt this kind of subterfuge.

Wherever you go you must impress her, through conversation, with your deep understanding of the human condition, your genuine longing for true fulfilment and your tragic loneliness owing to the fact that the world seems to be full of superficial people unable to understand your needs. Sure, there's no shortage of women willing to bed you (you mischievous man-of-the-world, you), but it hardly counts as the real thing, does it?

She will be expecting all this, and will then be expecting you to leap on her like a Catholic priest released from his vows after fifty years. She may even be more than willing to accommodate you in your apparent need to release the tensions caused by unrequited mental longing via the base and sweaty medium of sexual congress.

It is at this moment that you should look at your cards one last time. With one exception they have all been played. Now decide; what do you wish to do next? You can quite easily repair to bed with this lady. But tomorrow, or the day after, she will rapidly realise that you're the same as all the rest. If she doesn't come to that conclusion she will simply assume that you are a rather mixed-up weed beyond salvation and abandon you to the harsh but fair laws of nature, to be consumed by the pack at some future date.

There is no doubt that in her present emotional condition she will be an entirely satisfactory bedmate. Once. But true artists will know that by clever tactics they can procure an extremely satisfactory bedmate on any number of future occasions. This is achieved very easily.

Whatever else you may say or do this evening, do not, under any circumstances, lay a hand upon her person. You may caress her cheek briefly in that sensitive way of yours; run your fingers through her hair for a moment; hold her hand at moments of extreme emotional tension (which you will create in the conversation while discussing the noble, but thwarted nature of your emotions with regard to life in general and women in particular), and you may even kiss her gently on the cheek as you say goodnight. Indeed, a brief, but voluptuous kiss on the lips, combined with murmured thanks for all her understanding, may well be in order.

But that is all you will do. Today.

You will then wait at least a week before taking her somewhere exceptionally civilised. After which, it need not be said, you will take her back to your eyrie and administer the physical act which she is now more desirous of than she believes you to be with such ferocity that you will take her breath away and doubtless make her eyes pop out of her head. Because by now she wants to help you, you poor suffering lamb, and will begin to do so in the only material way she sees possible. She will continue to apply this kind of physical balm to your mental needs for some time; at least until she begins to feel that now is the time for you to reciprocate by acknowledging that she is the very person who can supply all the missing emotional ingredients which you listed on your first evening together. By now it will be a matter of pride with her that she can do so. She will allow you some latitude in recognising this, but eventually you will have to realise it and accept it, or lose her and be recognised for the bastard you indubitably are. The choice is yours . . .

One thing you cannot fail to have noticed throughout all this is that it does require a significant amount of private conversation. In order that you may achieve this you are commended to an accepted process whereby you take the lady out to dinner. This has a number of advantages, not least of which will be the facility with which you may hold conversations of a deeply intimate and romantic (not to say personal) nature in relative peace. Further you are given the opportunity to demonstrate your worldliness via your choice of venue, and the depth of your esteem which will vary in direct proportion to the size of the bill. Once again this latter is a thing which most women will deny, but you and I both know it's true. The size of your bank balance is just another of those little tests you have to go through.

Other benefits also accrue. You can, by your choice of venue, not only demonstrate your worldly knowledge, but also provide a suitably emotional (for which read romantic, for which read candle-lit) setting for your verbal assault.

Further opportunities present themselves as well. First you should pick a place which you are quite confident you can cope with without actually making a fool of yourself. There is no future in not being able to read or comprehend the menu, still less in refusing claret because you prefer red wine with your meal. And washing-up, so I hear, has few attractions to beautiful women anxious to keep their hands soft for those intimate moments later on.

On the other hand, although it may sound as if it comes straight out of a Roger Bond movie, bunging the head waiter a fiver before you take your seat is a most efficacious ruse. Explain to him how you have matters of great moment to discuss, and can't be troubled with dredging up your rusty French to deal with the menu. He will be pleased to explain it all (for *her* benefit, of course), and will doubtless be more than willing to suggest a truly magnificent wine in keeping with Madam's taste. All this will be doubly true should you indicate that there is another fiver where the first one came from should the evening meet with your approval.

It is also worth cultivating a restaurant on a regular basis. Good ones will not greet you with the old 'back again so soon?' blushmaker, but will be enthusiastic while remaining rewardingly discreet. Regular customers are always welcome and never embarrassed. Although I have been to one in which the manager arrived at a table I was sharing with a new but adorable young friend, wearing a sign round his neck which carried the legend 'You'll never get away with it'. This sort of thing must be avoided at all costs.

In truth the question of dining out, and the aphrodisiac qualities of various foods (and one or two other substances), is worthy of entirely separate consideration . . .

Aphrodisiacs and the Dangers of Over-Indulgence

Give me an ounce of civet, good apothecary, to sweeten my imagination
William Shakespeare, *King Lear*

Most boys, after they have graduated from looking up dirty words in the dictionary, move on to reading the underwear ads in women's magazines and from there to the hard stuff: D H Lawrence, James Joyce, whoever. It is quite normal for them to include in their steamy literary curriculum one or both of the ultimate pinnacles of pubescent eroticism – the *Kama Sutra* or *The Perfumed Garden*. Students of the latter tome may well have become enthralled with one recurring theme which was often invoked in order to sway the heart (and, more importantly, the body) of recalcitrant females. This was the love-philtre so beloved of alchemists (when they weren't trying to turn lead into gold) which produced dramatic and instantaneous results.

While it is an endearing thought aswarm with so many possibilities that most men believe in it because they would like to, there is little if any cause to imagine that any such thing as an infallible aphrodisiac really exists.

However, even though the hard truth may be less palatable than the myth there is still a certain amount of credence which we may successfully give to certain stimulants although their main effect, it must be said, is psychological. But since there is anyway an undoubted and noticeable effect to be gained from such concoctions we would do well to consider their nature and the best way in which they may be included in our repertoire.

By now we are assuming that you are past the stage of mumbling at women in the street and then wandering off nursing your frustration under a folded raincoat. Although you may not be an expert we assume that you at least are possessed of the temerity to effect introductions and make unrepeatable offers which no woman in her right mind would dream of refusing. By the same token we must believe that such offers are couched in reasonably civilised and sophisticated terms, and that you are well past the 'Hello darling, what about a fierce one?' level. Be that as it may you will find that there are women out there who will remain impervious to your cool charm, and may even be silly enough to turn down your offers. In which case it may help if you are able to bring some sort of aphrodisiac into play.

As we have said, these tend to be of a mainly psychological nature, whether they are swallowed, rubbed on or injected, and largely work on the creation of atmosphere in some way.

Given that an aphrodisiac, by whatever methods are applicable to its individual nature, relies on a mental effectiveness for its results you can see that there are occasions when perhaps the direct approach is the best. It is at moments like this when language is the best aphrodisiac going. You may use it to create a soft romantic atmosphere, rabbiting on endlessly about how beautiful she is, what lovely hair/eyes/skin/legs/shoulders/clothes/norks she possesses, hoping to charm her into your honey-trap. Or you may take another course. You could go for shock tactics, and this is often the best way. If she's a bit of a rough diamond then the slushy charm bit – to which hopefully she is unused – counts as shock treatment. If you think she's refined then go a bit coarse; take her slumming and let her see what a rootin' tootin' tough guy you are. Even, if you think it will pay off, try talking dirty. This is strictly for people playing the percentages, because if it works you're away and if it doesn't you get your face slapped, or possibly worse.

Although middle-of-the-road compromises are not usually recommended they may work here, since so much depends on your reading of her character, and there is so much to lose if you're wrong or unsure. Good halfway-house lines might be something like 'My mother said that if I wasn't in bed by midnight I should go home' or maybe 'You'd better get going or you'd better get going'.

Most girls know what you're about if you offer them breakfast, but in many business fields it is now accepted that a working breakfast is not unusual. Offer it by all means. If she says yes then ask her if you should call her or nudge her.

This sort of bluntness throws down a gauntlet which is reasonably challenging but not so clearly-defined that its offering or refusal will cause any offence or hard-feeling. But it does work. And it has the advantage that the intentions are clear and dishonourable on both sides right from the start, which can save a great deal of time for all concerned.

It is also true that aphrodisiacs may take a more concrete form than this, one well-tested variety being the small, but wildly expensive token of your 22-carat esteem. Now, while your pocket money may not run to huge extravagances it is well-known that pretty girls get minks the same way minks get minks. George Bernard Shaw it was, I believe, who spoke to a pretty girl for the first time one evening and offered her a small sum if she would go to bed with him. She refused, asking him what sort of girl he thought she was. He replied by offering her a million pounds if she would go to bed with him. She thought for a bit and then accepted. 'Right,' said Shaw, 'now that we've established what sort of girl you are we're only arguing about the price.'

In truth small gifts – perfume, flowers, chocolates, etc, thought they may work well enough (let's face it, the Yanks didn't do so bad with chewing gum and nylons during the war) don't really qualify as aphrodisiacs in any but the vaguest sense, although chocolate may be an exception. Let us regard the questions of ingested substances, into which category chocolate may rightfully be placed.

Taking a lady out to dinner is an established practice which we have previously mentioned in passing. You may be tempted to disregard it as being a bit overplayed and perhaps even somewhat passé, but don't write it off that quickly, since it has several attractions. Not least of these is the fact that it affords you a reasonably peaceful venue in which your personal charms can wreak their subtle magic. Providing you choose the right sort of place, that is, and avoid loud trendy establishments. Unless, of course, you already know the lady well enough to make conversation superfluous and wish only to barrage her with aphrodisiac concoctions which we shall deal with presently. Of course it is possible that you are a poor conversationalist yourself or that she is so dim it would be easier to have a meaningful discussion with Nelson's Column, in which case go right ahead and eat somewhere really noisy.

In any of these eventualities you will still be lucky enough to come to grips with the aphrodisiac potential afforded by all restaurants and one or two other places besides. Anyone who has seen the film *Tom Jones* will know at once that the simple act of eating is rife with a million opportunities for eroticism and erotic suggestion. Those who have also seen *The Thomas Crown Affair* will know that the game of chess is not without its merits, but that doesn't concern us here.

Aside from the suggestive fashion in which you cram your exotic grub into your face, or toy meaningfully with the wine bottle, you should know that some foods are actually very beneficial to the art of seduction. It is essential that over-indulgence is avoided at this level, since neither of you will be any use to the other if you're so bloated you can't walk, or worse still have to spend the major part of the night speaking to God on the big white telephone.

Provided that a modicum of restraint is applied, all should be well, however. You are doubtless already aware that certain foods have something of a reputation as far as aphrodisiacs are concerned, and you will know at once that hamburger and chips isn't on the list, which is another good reason for avoiding loud places. Or is it? We'll look at that again in a minute.

One of the principals on the list of rude food has always been shellfish of any sort, and oysters in particular. Quite why this should be so is not clear, and in view of the price of most kinds of shellfish (especially oysters) it is hard to avoid the suspicion that it could just be a rumour put about by the catering industry to increase sales, since there is little doubt that a great percentage of their trade consists of young gentlemen following the time-honoured pattern of wining and dining young girls who they hope will turn out not to be ladies after all.

But it seems that the rumour may perhaps contain a certain amount of truth. Indeed it may even be a truth which is not specifically confined to shellfish. Among the many wonders which modern science has recently turned up is one which bears directly upon this matter. It would appear that steak contains, among other things, a certain chemical which acts directly on a chemical present in the human brain under natural conditions. This natural chemical is the one responsible for, if you don't mind the simplification, your inhibitions. It's the one which holds you back all the time. As minute quantities of this are destroyed or overwhelmed by the chemical in steak so your inhibitions are also overcome. This, of course happens only in a very small way, and it would be unreasonable to expect a convent girl to turn into Gypsy Rose Lee after one good helping of châteaubriand but the effect is present and undeniable nonetheless. Which seems a good reason to talk your sweetheart into eating vast quantities of *steak tartare*, since this is served raw, and cooking does destroy the chemicals as well as the flavour.

This chemical effect is not only present in steak, however, but in all high-protein foods like meat, fish and cheese, which goes a long way to substantiating all those rumours about oysters, quite apart from the sensual implications rife in slipping the little chappies down your throat.

It would also seem to do a great service to the purveyors of hamburgers – or better still cheeseburgers – whether of the on-site or takeaway variety.

Even more interesting is the fact that swarthy continental types tend to eat a great deal of raw-ish meat, a lot of seafoods and some extremely unrefined (and horribly pungent) cheese, which perhaps would account for their exaggerated reputation as lovers.

Also in the chemical stakes we should include the inoffensive cocoa bean. This hitherto unremarkable vegetable also contains a chemical substance which, contrary to what we have just discovered, exists in the brain naturally, and rejoices in a triple-barrelled name with which we need not concern ourselves, mostly because I can't spell it.

In the everyday run of events this chemical exists only in small quantities and has little effect on your life. In moments of great tension it is released in substantial quantities and increases your pulse-rate, your breathing speed and doubtless opens your eyes wider as well. In fact it is this chemical which causes all the physical manifestations which lead spectators to believe that you are excited about something, mostly because you are. Also present, as we have said, in the cocoa bean, this chemical may safely be ingested via the inoffensive medium of chocolate, which makes the TV poofter in the black get-up less of a berk than you thought. Also it makes Easter Eggs and other confectionery gifts a more sensible investment than you may previously have believed them to be.

However, none of these things, admirable though they may be, can be said to have anything like a dramatic effect, and it is exactly this which we are striving for. Far more efficacious, and just as readily obtainable, is the simplest form of aphrodisiac in the world: alcohol.

Although overeating may temporarily incapacitate you, and even eventually make you fat and die of heart attacks, the danger of over-indulgence with booze is far greater. Apart from anything else, most people, and especially women, know their limits when it comes to nosh. Very few people of either sex are as sapient about drink.

As far as you are concerned the dangers are greatest. A little bit of Dutch courage is a wonderful thing, and may even be vital to the cause, but anything more than that is likely to have disastrous effects. Not least is the possibility that you will be driving home, and if you don't actually collect a piece of council furniture, such as a lamp-post or a Keep Left bollard, you still run the risk of losing your licence and spending the night in the slammer instead of your cosy love-nest. This is to be avoided at all costs, and if any doubt exists you should get a taxi.

Less opprobrious, but still undesirable, is the chance that you will drink so much that you will become clearly incapable, not to mention offensive. I have committed this grievous sin only once, and having assaulted the innocent commissionaire at a nightspot, in a vain attempt to steal his admittedly impressive headgear, proceeded to rant and rave most of the night. I was most surprised, not to mention fortunate, to find Madam still present the next day. If you do become muddy drunk the chances are that you won't be so lucky. You may find that even if she doesn't actually walk out on you then she will almost certainly decline any invitation to return home with you, and you can cancel all plans of a ferocious nature which you may have been entertaining. This, if it has no other benefits, will save you from distinguishing yourself in the manner of one of my colleagues, who puked on his lady friend within minutes of getting her into bed for the first time. There are few things which will more readily dampen a lady's ardour than being sick into her top pocket, so be warned.

Even if you are lucky enough to avoid this cataclysm there are still other pitfalls awaiting you, should you find yourself administering mouth-to-mouth resuscitation to a bottle of Southern Comfort prior to retiring to bed, and you may well find yourself totally incapable of administering anything else at all, never mind all your evil intentions. The famous droop has not won its reputation easily, and its path into legend is littered with the corpses of enthusiastic but flaccid suitors.

It would be far more acceptable if you could manage to

get Madam a little tipsy instead, and save your own over-indulgence for nights out with the boys.

And I do mean tipsy; it is no part of our plan to get her legless. There are other ways of making her lie down. Plus it is dead embarrassing in your favourite restaurant if you are seen struggling with an erstwhile demure young lass who is now as pissed as a parrot and anxious to fight the first person in the room who says hello. Women do have an occasionally fortunate habit of passing out when they're drunk, but at such moments they tend not to feel like indulging in anthing of an especially physical nature. While she may not mind if you do, it won't be that much fun, and you're bound to enjoy the whole thing a lot more with her active participation than without it.

What you're after here is to induce in her a happy state of amorous well-being. The moment at which she is in love with the whole world and you are the nearest representative of it is the moment to stop her drinking anything further.

While it may be hard for her to judge her own capacity for drinking it will be nigh on impossible for you to do so on her behalf. You will have to watch her very closely, although some women do not always exhibit the classic signs of incipient drunkenness. It will be far more valuable if you simply take note of how much she drinks, and whether she mixes it or not. More to the point you should try to regulate her drinking by pressing foaming tankards of vodka into her hand if she isn't doing that well or by steadfastly refusing to notice when she starts licking the inside of her empty glass if she's had too much.

At this point you should take account of how long the evening is going to last. If you have plenty of time you needn't get her ratted inside the first 10 minutes. She'll probably pass out later if you do. And remember that strong drink has unpredictable results on all of us if it is swilled down very quickly, so there is no sense in ordering her a large Scotch in a straight glass right off.

The best plan is to encourage her to sup a cocktail or two and then a modicum of wine with the meal, plus maybe a liqueur if the occasion and her sobriety calls for it.

Cocktails, you will recall, are mixes of fruit juice and alcohol originally devised in the States during prohibition in an attempt to disguise the truly appalling taste of some of the rougher brands of moonshine available at the time. In the scheme of things you are dealing with they also serve to conceal the staggering quantities of different alcoholic beverages which can successfully be contained in a single drink without blinding or killing the recipient. This sneaky device will serve to circumnavigate the fact that most girls will be aware that trying to get them drunk is a major weapon in every seducer's armoury. With luck many of them will be unaware of the old adage about not mixing grain and grape, and will thus gladly bang off a couple of Killer Zombies (which look and taste like the product of a WI flower-arranging class but contain phenomenal amounts of rum) and wash their meal down with some fairly hefty swipes at a light and fruity white wine. The application of a potent liqueur (which may be disguised to good effect in one of those nancy coffees which look and taste like hot Guinness) ought to set the seal on the whole event. At worst it will render her susceptible to the offer of a nightcap at your place, and if she begins to suspect that your plans do not include the wearing of any night-time apparel whatever, least of all a cap, she probably won't mind at all by now. If she does, a substantial brandy when you get in ought to work wonders.

There are, naturally enough, various other kinds of substances which their supporters claim will have an aphrodisiac effect, and most of these, being of a suspicious if not illegal nature, are best taken in the privacy of your own home, or that of someone you know very well. Even, in extremes, in the home of someone you don't know that well, but who you are still certain is not actually a member of the constabulary.

Most common of these is the product known variously as marijuana, grass, shit, dope, weed, hash and still occasionally (by late sixties leftovers) as pot. The rights and wrongs of this situation have no place in these pages, so we shall ignore them. It must be pointed out that you are risking a short spell as one of Her Majesty's guests should you choose to indulge, and that therefore a degree of circumspection must be employed.

After that you may smoke it in pipes, roll it in cigarettes or bake it in cakes. There are other highly-specialised ways of getting it into your system, but these are the most common. The effect is almost universally the same, and although deep states of perceptual awareness are not common, the drug does induce a pleasant, if not intimate state of contentment which provides an excellent backdrop to bedroom adventuring. It may also lend a certain dream-like quality to the event which many people will find eminently pleasurable. Unlike alcohol it will not make you fighting mad and neither will it afflict you with a loss of bodily powers. For these reasons it is at least as efficacious as a bottle of Chablis and in many cases even preferable.

Like marijuana there are other drugs available to aid this mental surrender to hedonism and, like grass, they are nearly always taken in conjunction with booze rather than instead of it. Perhaps the second most common (after dope) is the drug of the nouveau bourgeoisie. Sometimes discreetly called Charlie, and also by a variety of other humorous names, cocaine is the socially acceptable drug of the eighties in many quarters. Once again it is illegal, and you must examine your own conscience, not mine, before you decide what to do about it. The use of this drug will make you witty, intelligent, attractive, good-looking, and fun to be with. It also stimulates physical desire in some people (but not others) while its anaesthetic effect is quite liable to numb your extremities without preventing their use. This seems to be a highly desirable property.

While over-indulgence in marijuana will cause you to float up to the ceiling before going to sleep at once, excessive ingestion of coke (or granulated money as it is sometimes known) will have quite the opposite effect. Try not to assault anyone you know.

Uppers – purple hearts, drinamyl, sulph, speed, whatever you want to call it – will have a similar vitalising effect to that of cocaine. As a rule it will also make you sweaty, shivery, thirsty and want to wee a great deal. As a side-effect it may also make your willy shrink into invisibility, but this shouldn't be a problem, since it will also depress your sex-drive to the point where you'd turn down a foursome with Debbie Harry, Kate Bush and Felicity Kendal.

While we are still in the league of straightforward chemical stimulants we come again to the love-philtre with which we began. There are any number of such things commercially available. Ginseng is perhaps the most common, and though it is simply sold as a sort of natural tonic, it is often claimed to have dramatic powers as a sexual stimulant. There are as many detractors of this point of view as there are supporters, and it would once again appear that you're on your own in this.

We can offer you a little more advice when it comes to the frighteningly expensive confections like Love Pearls or Love Sugar (which tend to have no noticeable effect whatever) and the more famous Spanish Fly. This stuff, which is brewed from insects as the name implies, has developed quite a reputation over the years and although this is not without just cause it's not that straightforward either. To begin with, few of the overpriced substances sold as Spanish Fly actually contain the genuine article in any quantity, if at all. Consequently their effect, if present, is entirely psychological, which needn't be all bad.

The real thing actually acts upon the body chemically to produce a reaction in the urinary tract manifested as a cross between a burning sensation and an itch. This convinces, people that they are overwhelmed with physical desire and they at once try to relieve the itch by, um, scratching it. If you could get hold of the real thing it would probably work a treat.

There are also a number of substances which you may apply to the relevant portions of your anatomy which will produce the same effect. These are not to be confused with the 'delay-spray' creams and aerosols which retard the critical moment. This action relies on a mild anaesthetic not unlike that which trainers spray on wounded footballers, while the others, the stimulant variety, rely on a heat-inducing substance which you will find present in rheumatism treatments like Ralgex and are usually detectable from their pronounced and rather horrific odour. Much the same sort of effect can be obtained at far less cost from a number of household products, and you wouldn't be the first person who's rubbed Vick on their naughty bits. Be warned that the results aren't immediately discernible and the stuff, being greasy, doesn't wash off that easy, so don't bung handfuls of it around unless you want your genitalia to resemble the Blackpool illuminations.

More to the point with all of this is the fact that it's not you we're trying to arouse, it's Madam, and you can hardly apply a succession of aromatic creams to her person and hope that she will remain blind to your intentions.

And although it may be quite within the rules of the game that you should try to persuade her to imbibe more alcohol than is good for her virtue, it is most decidedly the act of a cad to slip young girls a mickey in the hope that all resistance will fade into obscurity forthwith. In other words do not bung drugs of any sort into her food or drink without first seeking her permission and approval.

If by now you have got her home and into a happy state of relaxation you may care to try further ploys in order to win her favour. Soft lighting is indubitably a favourite here, as almost everybody looks like Paul Newman in the dark. This is especially recommended if you suffer from acne or warts and even more so if you are remarkable ugly. In fact in the latter case you may be well advised to take both your and her consumption of alcohol to excess. That way if she passes out on you then at least you'll be able to make the best of a bad job, (which could well be a better result than you'd have obtained if her *mentis* had remained substantially *compos*), and if you pass out then you won't be conscious enough to mourn her simply passing.

Music is a good standby as well. Turning the box on is usually a no-no, but records will do wonders. It is not even necessary to reduce yourself to the level of romantic schmaltz courtesy of Sacha Distel or Des O'Connor; almost anything will do, although the softer it is the better. And there are more than a few excellent compilation albums around which are loaded with the tenderest love songs the pop world has produced, so you can even stay true to type and retain your integrity.

If you're lucky enough (and wealthy enough) you can even induce a more exotic and erotic mood by inviting her to partake of your home sauna/sunbed/jacuzzi or whatever. Any or all of these things are definitely useful to you, and may even suffice as the prime reason for her presence in your mountaintop hideaway, especially during the daylight hours. An invitation to sample one of these delights could well be attractive enough to lure her there, and once there they may prove sufficiently stimulating as to make all other forms of aphrodisiac redundant, which can be no bad thing.

It is, of course, highly unlikely that you will possess any of this esoteric and self-indulgent junk, in which case you can't operate the ploy. Unless, that is, you are smart enough to realise that there are any number of commercial concerns who offer services of this nature to the general public. It is certainly true that many sports establishments – squash clubs and similar – include a sauna or a sunbed or a jacuzzi, or any combination of the three within the premises. The effect on involved parties will be roughly the same as it would be in your own home, although perhaps not as pronounced. All you have to do is make sure that you whisk her out of the door ASAP and get her back home to your place for a refreshing drink of freshly-squeezed orange juice (liberally topped up with Campari) before the effect wears off or some other smart bastard moves in and queers your pitch.

Many of the nicer hotels include a swimming pool and sports facility of this nature, and if you can't get her to stay in one overnight with you then at least find the nearest and become a member so you can while away pleasant days with her at your side. Poolside drinks, a swim, a sauna, sunbed, a jacuzzi, even a massage if the hotel or club can offer it – and we don't need to snigger at that, do we? – and then away home. You know it makes sense.

All these things are the sensual pleasures of the flesh, and you will do no harm at all to cultivate them like fury. The results will more than repay the effort. There is, in London, an establishment known as The Sanctuary, which excels at this sort of sensual pampering, and ladies leaving its portals look radiantly beautiful, glowing with an inner rapture which it is a joy to behold. This is, sadly, an exclusively feminine preserve, and men are not allowed in. No matter, since it is not you we are trying to seduce. Send her to such a place. It is a thoughtful and charming gift in any event. All you have to do is make sure you're the one who collects her afterwards. You will be stunned and pleased with the result. Then take her home for dinner. Do not go to a restaurant. Do not turn the box on. Cook her something subtle and erotic. Not too spicy, but tasty. Prawn brochettes, say. Then give her plenty of nice things to drink, stuff the chocolate-coated after-dinner mints down her throat, put your sexiest music on the turntable in a darkened room and she won't be able to resist your advances. Promise. Well, up to a point . . .

Even now our repertoire, though extended, is still not exhausted. For instance. Here's a short history lesson. In the good old days in Rome, when Max Bygraves was only a lad, the ruling classes used to stage huge shows, known as Circuses. Nothing at all like the sort of offering we are accustomed to seeing from Billy Smart on Boxing Day, these events were the opiate of the masses. It took their minds off unemployment and the Danegeld, which was a sort of Roman equivalent of VAT. During these shows, if you can call them that, vast numbers of innocent animals and people met horrible and grisly fates. This is something I'm sure you knew. What you may not have known, because you didn't read your Tacitus like a good lad when you were at school, is that the effect of all this bloodletting on even the most noble of Roman ladies was to induce a state of great sexual excitement. The young lads of Rome used to hang about the entrance to the Circus Maximus until they spotted a likely-looking hysteric and then make sure they sat next to her. Once the excitement rose to the right pitch they were assured of a pleasant grope if nothing else.

While I would hesitate to suggest that you go around killing people simply in order to get your rocks off, let me advise you to watch the wrestling on the box on Saturday afternoons. See the people doing all the shouting in the audience? All the screaming and getting completely carried away by the thrill and brutality of it all? Women.

Anything which involves danger – motorsport, say – or physical combat like wrestling, boxing or rugby, or even musclebound heroes charging around in a minimum of clothing, like athletics, is liable to produce a similar sort of reaction in certain women, and more of them than you think or will ever admit it. There are even some women (only a few, thank God) who cause aggro in pubs and discos simply in order to enjoy the spectacle of two men fighting for their favours. A lot of the time they go off with the victor, and never mind that you've just had your head sawn off on her account, so be careful how you pick them. It is, nevertheless, a phenomenon worthy of note and exploitation.

This reaction doesn't only manifest itself in bloodletting. Pop concerts are justifiably renowned for this sort of thing. Whether it's the continual pounding beat at high volume (which also makes the floor and seats vibrate in sympathy), or the overt sexuality of the hip-swinging idols waving their disgustingly symbolic guitars about the place is hard to say. It is still a commonplace that young girls wet themselves in excitement and older girls wet themselves for entirely different reasons. It is not unusual for demented female fans to remove their knickers and chuck them at the artists in moments of extreme tension. If you get the chance, take a woman to see someone loud and aggressive and observe the truth for yourself.

Alternatively you could go alone and try to attach yourself to an unaccompanied young lady. She will almost certainly be in a suitably frenzied condition and you will probably be able to avail yourself of her charms with a minimum of effort. In fact it is at moments like this when the no-nonsense direct approach is most likely to meet with unqualified success.

There is still not an end to this, since you will find, if you speak with more than a few women, that they will all retain some sort of fantasy at the end of which some superhuman being gets his hands on the goodies. These daydreams are very often of a highly complex nature, which renders guessing a difficult and risky business. It is of far more value if you can discover in advance the nature of any such fantasy and then, after a suitable interval (spontaneity is vital and scheming machinations a turn-off), allow it to be enacted, casting yourself in the role of the aforesaid lucky blighter who makes off with her virtue.

Remember what we have said about all these rape fantasies women are supposed to entertain, and do not be misled into thinking you can get away with it; you can't. Dressed in black leather from head to toe, and creeping through her bedroom window in the middle of the night, you will be as welcome as a coffin at a wedding.

But still. Maybe she fancies being seduced on a billiard table, in which case all you have to do is install one in your living room and invite her round for a couple of frames. Doesn't matter who breaks first. Or perhaps she'd like to do it on an aeroplane or a train, in which case go and see your travel agent at once. If it's the back seat of a Roller – go hire one and give her a nice surprise. Don't forget to run out of petrol on the way home from the restaurant.

There are many things of a similar ilk which crop up from time to time, and it is up to you to capitalise on them and enjoy them. Let's face it, you'll be making two people happy, which must qualify as your good deed for the day. Look on it as a kind of charitable work, an act of kindness.

Remember that when you are dealing with people's fantasies you are also messing with their dreams, which are fragile little items and must be handled accordingly. In many cases you will find that this sort of activity is better left until you know the lady fairly well. Intimately, even. Before you start to involve yourself in intricacies of this nature you should perhaps pay a little more attention to the basics. You don't want to screw it all up before you've screwed it up, do you? No, quite right you don't. You've gone to a lot of trouble already to smarten yourself up, go out and find the right lady, sweep her off her feet with your charm and a bunch of flowers and then ply her with a variety of expensive stimulants, not to mention hiring the Halle Orchestra to play a serenade in the living room while you, dressed like Steve Davis and clutching a bowl of prawns, fight it out with Big Daddy on the fitted carpet.

The time now, before you begin indulging her wildest dreams, is ripe for you to whisk her off into unheard of transports of sexual ecstasy of a more banal manner. But first, you must learn some manners . . .

Bedside Manners

Come up and see me sometime
Mae West, *Diamond Lil*

So then, here you both are, chez vous or, come to that, chez anyone you know who just happens to be away for a few days. Question is, now you've got her where she wants you, what are you going to do about it?

It's a perennial question which crops up every year, this, and one which is common to a number of areas, not all of which need be connected with the subject in hand. I can recall a time when it afflicted Arsenal to such an extend that even die-hard supporters (and believe me, Arsenal supporters do die hard) despaired of them. It's the question of finishing power. Time after time they'd bring the ball right up to the goalmouth and then spend 10 minutes kicking it around among themselves before finally making a desultory pass right into the arms of the defending goalkeeper.

Arsenal's answer came in the shape of Charlie George, and though it's hard to see just who is going to save England from the same fate it is still true to say that football teams can sort out this kind of problem a whole lot easier than you can. Apart from anything else, you don't have three million pounds to spend on transfer fees, and even if you did it wouldn't do you any good, because the object here is to keep you on the winning team, not transfer you off it and let some other smart-alec superstar have all the glory and rewards. Not to mention all the smart tarts.

In many cases you will already, by virtue of your skilful handling of the situation, whether it be long-term or a crash-course, have created a situation in which she wants all the same things that you do. This is the bottom line, and is exactly what you have been trying to achieve all evening with your smooth patter and vast expenditure on alcoholic beverages of unparalleled toxicity.

If everything has worked out according to your master plan then the final move of transferring your activities from the living room into the bedroom should be simple enough. She will, by all those signs of body-talk, deep breathing and flashing eyes, not to mention languidly stretched legs, already have indicated as much to you, and it only remains to you to make that last suggestion. You know, the one about how you'd be more comfortable lying down, or how your chateau-bottled lemonade tastes better when consumed in a horizontal position and isn't the floor hard? Or the bit about 'Do you know the difference between making love and making conversation? No? Then lie down, I want to talk to you.' Ask yourself: has she seen the truly astounding pattern on your bedroom ceiling? Then ask her the same question. And does she know that there's a haggis nest in the tree outside your bedroom window but unfortunately it's only visible if you put your head on the pillow and close your eyes?

And how about that truly phenomenal pillow you've just bought, made entirely from the fur of the sea-otter? If you lie down and close your eyes you can hear the surf pounding in the distance. Or maybe it's just the blood rushing to her head.

You could, on the other hand, be direct. Lean across and look earnestly into her eyes and then ask her to come to bed. Alternatively, and even more earnestly, you could just tell her she's beautiful and that you want to make love. Suggesting that you both ought to make beautiful music together with the minimum possible delay is a bit outré, as is just blurting out 'Let's screw'.

You could tell her, if you think that you're a convincing enough actor, that you've just discovered from your specialist that you are suffering from an unknown disease which is baffling scientists the world over, and that you've only got a few weeks to live, maximum. Which is why you really want to screw her before you die. While this is a ploy which is unlikely to meet with unqualified success, or even a great deal of credulity, its humorous value may be enough to carry the day for you, and even the night as well – you should be so lucky.

Whatever you do, don't tell her that she's the most wonderful thing that ever happened to you. The best that can happen is she'll laugh, and the worst is that she'll believe you, which will present huge difficulties for both of you.

Ostentatious yawning is likewise out of the question. It serves no useful purpose other than to make her think that she bores you to death, and could well result in her precipitate departure before you've had a chance to mention the fascinating reproduction David Hockney original prints decorating the walls of your boudoir.

In the end there are any number of ways to lead a lady astray from the path of virtue and directly onto the path which leads to your bed, and by now you ought to be in a position to spot such openings as they crop up in conversation. To be honest this sort of thing will be almost entirely redundant nine times out of 10, especially if you have been steamily engaged in the sort of heavy groping which would give the Festival of Light a coronary were it to be televised (even in soft focus) for the past hour and a half.

Because this, of course, is the most heavily trodden path into a bedroom. The brushing of the cheek, the tender kisses, the soulful stares, all of these will eventually give way to frenzied grappling, bearhugs which would squeeze the breath out of Rocky Marciano and then desperate struggles with reams and reams of seemingly unnecessary undergarments.

Following on all this it will be more natural to retire into the comfort and privacy of the bedroom than to stay where you are or call a cab and send her home. Unless . . . no, we've asked that question already. This does not mean that there's anything wrong with staying where you are and completing your coupling on the carpet. Few things could be more natural. But then again, beds are, generally speaking, more comfortable, unless yours would give a Trappist Monk backache, in which case buy a new one.

Whatever course you decide to follow will be that which seems most natural and obvious. If your groping on the floor comes at the conclusion of a long and hard-fought campaign, and you have reason to suspect that breaking the mood – even for a few seconds – by changing venue could undo your good work and do up all those buttons, stay where you are. If that is not the case then you should be perfectly justified in moving to a more luxurious location. We'll come back to the carpet-shaggers and their friction-burnt knees and elbows in a while. First let's deal with the transition to the bedroom.

To begin with we should ensure that the room itself is correctly prepared. If you left home this evening after hours of preparing yourself for one or two moments of glory you would have been foolish in the extreme if you had overlooked the obvious possibility that your bedroom was about to be subject to a fairly intimate test. In fact the whole house is about to get a good look over, so you should have taken a few elementary precautions.

It goes without saying that these will have included the acquisition of adequate stocks of wine or other refreshment, all correctly chilled. You won't be silly enough to run out of milk, sugar, coffee or tea either, will you?

Nor will you have been dumb enough to leave embarrassing traces of previous adventures or misdemeanours lying around. There will not be 10 days' washing up all over the kitchen, or a horrid mess in the living room left behind after you finished your open-heart surgery experiments on the budgie. Nor will there be threatening communications from the bank about your overdraft left where they are visible. The same goes for those 'Don't leave the country' letters from credit companies and heartrending communiqués from 36 delectable ladies who have loved and lost.

And while it may be true to say it is better to have loved your wife than never to have loved at all you won't leave her picture on top of the goggle-box, will you?

The bedroom is an area you should look at even more

carefully than the rest of the house, but don't let that tempt you into skimping the overall job. Women have a staggeringly keen eye for detail and probably take more notice of little things – like lipstick rings on dirty wine glasses – than they do of big things.

However, you must still think more carefully about the bedroom than anywhere else. Before you go out make sure that the room will be at an equable temperature when you get home. While it is undesirable, and even uncomfortable, to maintain a bedroom at the same temperature as a living room it is equally, if not more detrimental to let it degenerate into an Arctic condition. No one wants icicles forming on their toes overnight and besides it is hard work being passionate in sub-zero conditions. Anyway, you know what they say about brass monkeys and cold weather.

In similar vein you should try to leave a little ventilation in your bedroom by means of a marginally open window. You don't want it to smell like a locker-room or a toilet, still less like a gin-palace. And make the bed. Not many people relish the prospect of batting on a sticky wicket. Women's lib may well involve making the man sleep on the wet patch, but there are limits.

And if you can't actually tidy the room up that well you should at least clear a path to the side of the bed so that you don't both have to step over piles of rubble and a half-built bookcase on your way to the land of your dreams. Nor will it do you any favours if the room is liberally sprinkled with assorted items of feminine lingerie, even if they do belong to your mum/sister who stayed with you last night. Expect her to believe that old rubbish? Get rid of lipsticks or other items of make up, perfume you wouldn't dream of wearing except to one of those odd discos you keep reading about in Sunday supplements, and anything else of a vaguely female disposition.

While you may not feel it necessary to make love in the dark in our enlightened age, you (and probably she as well) will quite possibly not relish the prospect of performing beneath the glare of a two million candlepower spotlight, so make sure that you have one source of light (preferably operated from the bedside) which will not be a serious rival to the sort of equipment employed by air-sea rescue services.

At the same time you may feel that it is an advantage to have some means of providing musical entertainment in the room. Once again we are not anticipating broadcasting to the Antipodes, so anything of a modest but effective nature – like a clock radio or a portable cassette – will do the trick. In the end radios are best, because it will mean that you won't have to interrupt the flow of your concentration to turn the record or tape over when it finishes.

Reading all this it would be easy to form the belief that your whole house and especially the bedroom should look like something out of a Habitat catalogue. This is not necessary. In fact most rooms and houses will look much more pleasant if there are at least a few traces of a personality (preferably yours and not the divorcee's next door) scattered about the place. You know the sort of thing; your old boxing/karate/kung fu trophies (which you can pick up dead cheap in almost any junk shop), Christmas cards from P McCartney and similar (pick your season carefully before you write these) and perhaps a letter offering you the job of Director-General of the BBC (you can do wonders with a photocopying machines these days). Of course if you know anything at all about the lady in question in advance then you will be able to decide upon the nature of this kind of artefact in advance also. Literary-minded girls will of course be far more susceptible to signed first editions than autographed copies of Adam and the Ants' latest vinyl offering, but you can work those sort of details out for yourself I'm sure.

Meanwhile the stage is set and ready for action, and you will have found a suitable means of manoeuvering her ladyship into the bedroom. If this should come about as a natural conclusion to a nightcap which has already taken on something of a physical demeanour then your next step will be simple enough, since you will both subside gracefully onto the bed and continue to allow events to run their normal course.

All too often this is not the case. You will generally find that either you haven't begun to grapple or that the act of movement will break the flow of whatever mood you have managed to establish so far. There is also a good chance, especially if you've been drinking at all, that one or both of you will need the use of the bathroom first. In any case this is a most sensible precaution, since it will save you having to make your excuses and leave at a later and perhaps more critical moment.

Having done this, and since you are now on your feet with the impetus slightly interrupted, it will do no harm to replenish drinks all round, and charge your glasses for later consumption. I seem to recall hearing that making love is something like the equivalent of a four mile run, so it isn't very surprising to discover that it makes most people a bit thirsty. Having a drink handy will save you getting up at the very moment when you'd rather stay exactly where you are.

Sweeping majestically through the portals of your bedchamber you will then find that both of you are standing around looking at the bed, and a further burst of finishing power is once again called for. You have several options. You may resume (or commence) a passionate embrace and then move easily and naturally into that bit where you subside onto the bed and the camera dissolves into shots of waves crashing onto rocky sea-shores while you get your jollies in discreet privacy (unless it's a Ken Russell film), or you may choose to adopt a somewhat more prosaic approach.

Lying on your bed, see, it's not only acceptable, but expected that you should rip each other's clothes off, casting them aside with a carelessness which bespeaks untold quantities of unbridled passion and lust. This can be fun and imposes no restrictions of etiquette upon either party. However it is generally the stuff of which dreams and films are made. In the films it is quite simple to stop the camera when the struggle to remove startlingly fashionable but subcutaneous clothing becomes more than a trifle undignified and resume at an opportune moment. This is not possible in real life except by mutual agreement.

Realists among us will accept quite readily that there are certain kinds of female garments which cannot be easily removed, even by their owner; attempting to do this while lying down on a bed with your mouth glued to hers and one hand trapped underneath her admittedly sylph-like form is the stuff of which great comedy films are made. Likewise it is not the simplest thing in the whole world to try removing your own shoes and socks while in the same position. Not only is it demonstrably uncool, it is a process which could involve considerable amounts of personal grief, and the last thing you want right now is a double hernia.

In view of all this it will frequently become necessary to interrupt the proceedings in order to deal with stubborn articles of clothing. This doesn't matter as long as you know how to deal with it. The rules are simple. She put the damn things on, and she knows you'll never get them off unaided, so get her to help you or do it herself while you take care of your leopardskin jumpsuit, you trendy little poof.

Even this is bound to involve an unseemly amount of writhing about and waving legs in the air, and there are few things less erotic than a pair of adult human beings impersonating the actions of a beached whale. This being so you may find that it is preferable to get shot of the clothes (or most of them) in advance, and leave your infighting to later.

This is not as easily managed as you may think. You cannot simply frogmarch her into the bedroom, indicate your side of the bed and show her where to put her clothes and then strip off. It lacks, you see, a certain amount of finesse, however practical a solution it may seem to be. In similar vein you should dismiss from your mind the idea that while she is in the bathroom you just fling your clothes aside, pile into bed and then invite her to join you when she emerges by the expedient of shouting at her from your position of repose.

You are better advised to allow your preliminary gropings to go far enough to arouse you both to the point of no return (after she starts the heavy breathing but prior to the screams of ecstasy) and then gently suggest that you'd be better off

in bed. This will give you both the chance to remove your outer clothing with dignity, before climbing between the sheets clad only in the male and female versions of scanty underclothes. And not only will this practical approach spare your blushes, it will also allow you to partake of one of life's greater pleasures; watching a woman undress. Vast numbers of entrepreneurial types have made staggering fortunes exploiting the attractions of this via the medium of establishments known in the coarse vernacular as strip clubs. You will now be able to reap all the benefits of such a place without the drawbacks of having to cough up the lolly for the entrance fee and the privilege of paying a fiver for a glass containing insufficient Scotch to drown a fly (in which species of animal life the joint will almost certainly abound). Furthermore you will be in the privileged position of being able to break the Prime Directive of strip clubs: the 'Don't touch the exhibits' rule.

You will, of course, extract your voyeuristic pleasure less than overtly while you remove your own clothes, since few people relish the act of putting on a private performance of this nature, even for someone with whom they are about to share the ultimate intimacy, at least to begin with. Later maybe, but not yet. Look, then, but don't stare. And if you do get caught looking it will be singularly appropriate for you to murmur something along the lines of 'You're a very beautiful woman' or similar.

Note that earlier in the proceedings, when you were meeting or wining and dining, this kind of creeping would have deservedly won you the grand order of the bum's rush, but now it is quite acceptable. Desirable, even, since it is exactly the sort of thing which all women want to hear, especially when they've got no clothes on. So desirable is it that you may even find it useful to murmur it appreciatively even if you don't get caught looking.

Unexpected compliments often work well, particularly at this advanced stage of your relationship, and may even be put to good use at an earlier stage. Stop the car while you're driving and just kiss her without speaking before you carry on driving towards your eyrie and her Waterloo. Interrupt her while she's speaking and do the same or tell her she's lovely. Make sure that you don't fall into the trap of not paying attention to what she was saying, mind. Women get cross about that sort of thing. This ploy will work well, but it is more relevant as you get nearer to your appointment with true lust; later rather than sooner is the rule with this.

You should now be dressed only in the briefest of attire, the pair of you. The time is now ripe, therefore, to get into bed. Some women are naturally shy, at least to begin with, and you will find that getting in to bed rather than on to it will suit them better. Others won't mind either way unless it's mid-December. There is, sadly, no way to tell in advance and you will just have to see how she feels about this. Right now, as in all matters which pertain only to questions of personal taste without interceding between you and the final objective, you should give her as many options as you can and try to follow her lead. The trick here is to make her feel as comfortable and as relaxed as you can.

Unless you are confronted with a woman who is responding simply to the animal in you both, who is with you only because of her desire for that bit of rough, or just looking for her grats with a macho superguy (in which case forget all the niceties and rip her clothes off as fast as you can) the best thing you can do is take your time. Let's face it, you want to have something to remember when you're 65, don't you? Right. And so does she. So give both of you the chance to allow all that takes place to sink gently into your unconscious and become imprinted on your brain. Who knows? She may go to work tomorrow and tell all her friends that you're a really excellent lover and thus start them queueing up for your favours. This is infinitely preferable to being written off as an out-and-out bastard not worth the time of day.

In these situations establishing a mild reputation as a seducer of young girls can do you big favours; it presents you as something of a challenge and may well open avenues of conquest which would have remained closed had not everybody been talking about your naughty habits. There's nothing as odd and unfathomable as human nature, and if you're the sort of person every girl's mother has been warning her against you could reap an immense harvest.

Having leapt into or onto bed with the lady in question you will now find that removing such flimsy garments as remain to you both is a task which can safely be accomplished without the embarrassing contortions mentioned previously. As a word of interest you may feel it worth considering that in many cases it is infinitely preferable to leave the odd flimsy wisp of silk or nylon to play with, rather than stripping naked straight off. Undressing a lady, even if it is only a token gesture, is an especially pleasurable and erotic experience which will serve to heighten the pleasure in your coupling rather than detract from it. This is, therefore, a pleasure (and a privilege) which you should not deny yourself or her. At this moment, as at all others along the way, your purpose must be to extract the maximum rather than the mimimum from everything you do. Remember that she is a woman and there to be enjoyed. You will do both of you a great disservice should you choose to skimp anything which you may regard as non-essential and plunge straight on to the heart of the matter.

Taking a lady to bed is not simply a question of sticking it in and wiggling it about. The delights are manifold, and you must strive to nourish and sample all of them, otherwise you are wasting everybody's time.

However all this is a question of techique of an extremely personal nature, and it is only right and proper that we should now draw a veil over the proceedings. Cut to soft-focus shots of crashing waves and dynamited factory chimneys . . .

Picture the scene. You're lying together, sated. Gently she leans over, nibbles your ear, says 'Hello big boy. Now I know why they call you superstud.' You smile modestly, kiss her gently but firmly on the lips before you both fall into a deep and dreamless sleep, locked in each other's arms. In the morning when you awake . . .

This will happen to you twice in your life, maybe three times if you're lucky. It is the vision of love perpetuated by Hollywood and the Barbara Cartlands of this world which has no place in the scheme of reality. You have, like so many others, been betrayed by the film industry, and will doubtless count your own sweaty unions as something of a failure by comparison. Don't worry. Let's regard the truth of the matter for a minute or two.

You're lying together, knackered, and wheezing gently like an LMR locomotive after a particularly prolonged puff. You're both drenched in a special sort of sweat which is concocted from a mixture of very hot water and something unpleasant but sticky, like marmalade. You've got cramp in one leg and your left arm has gone to sleep. You're as thirsty as a dehydrated camel and busting for a wee. Far from nibbling your earlobe, she is similarly bathed in sweat and her left elbow is gradually drilling through your ribcage and is on the point of piercing your liver and pinning it to the mattress. In all probability she's got cramp in muscles she didn't know she owned, as well. That'll teach you to attempt silly positions recommended in sex manuals.

Two possibilities present themselves. Either you keep quiet and die the sort of painful, lingering death which would have made the practitioners of the Inquisition rub their hands together in delight, or you do something to adjust the situation.

Eventually the pain will reach a point at which inactivity will become totally impossible and you will be forced to move. As you do so make up your mind; are you spending the night together, or is one of you going home?

If it is the latter then this is the moment to say something like 'My God, is that the time?' This is best done as soon as possible before either of you fall asleep or she gets the erroneous impression that you're staying exactly where you are. In every case the situation is much simplified if you are the one who has to leave. You are granted any number of reasons – like a change of clothing, shave, important meeting in Eastbourne early tomorrow – for taking your leave. You can use the last as a reason for removing her from your premises, or perhaps something like the fact that important business visitors are joining you for a working breakfast at home come first sparrow-chirp.

If none of these reasons apply then you will have to be more inventive, but before you move on to the realms of the improbable if not the downright impossible you must again make a choice. If you want her out, no questions and no return fixture then the more implausible the reason for her departure the better. If no such urgency presents itself then you can do no harm in staying where you are. In fact you could do considerable good.

Imagine she's staying, or you are, depending upon whose premises you are currently occupying. You will still have to disentangle yourself from your current position before you lose the use of both legs from gangrene or whatever obnoxious diseases cramp can cause. If you are playing at home then the drink of whatever you have thoughtfully provided will be readily to hand. Even this may not totally save you from disaster, since it is true that almost all women want a cuddle the moment you've found the only cold spot in the bed. Unless you wish to alienate her entirely, and earn her eternal disapprobation, you have no alternative but to comply with her wishes. You may find that you are the sort of person who relishes a cuddle at moments like these yourself, in which case there won't be a problem.

Nine times out of 10 you will find that women choose this particular moment to visit the bathroom, which is a polite way of describing the various necessary girl-things which some of them may wish or need to do. This means that you will be left alone for a while, only to be shortly confronted with an ice-cold body which wishes to entwine itself with yours in a joyous expression of togetherness. You have, as a polite gentleman, no alternative but to endure this. Indeed you are obliged to give every indication of enjoyment. Grit your teeth and you will find it relatively easy.

Before you go to sleep make sure that you have made polite enquiries as to the necessary time of arising, and that your alarm is set in plenty of time. It is not enough to simply add on the time you expect her to spend in the bathroom and set the clock that much earlier. Women can spend hours in bathrooms, expecially in the morning, and you will have to make allowance for this. You will also need to allow time for at least a modicum of intimacy prior to getting out of bed. Even if you have no plans to repeat your stupendous performance of tonight you will still need to spend some time in physical contact of a sort, and you would be silly if you didn't allow at least half an hour for this sort of thing.

Getting out of bed *à deux* is a feat fraught with almost as many pitfalls as getting into it, and also with as many pleasures. You would be abdicating your responsibilities if you chose to ignore them. If you both have to go to work then much of this must needs be eliminated from the calendar of events unless you wish to arise with the lark (and believe me, larks get up naffing early in the morning) and you will thus have to decide how much of it should rightfully be allowed to fall by the wayside. With luck, however, tomorrow will be a day of rest, and you may happily give yourself over to the indulgence of all the selfish and mutual pleasures inherent in having a woman about the place when you awake.

The first of these is the awakening ritual; the pleasant and mildly passionate embrace, the remembrance of all that has passed the night before and the shared intimacy of reliving such experiences together in an unspoken but communicable way. Then comes breakfast, or at least coffee, in bed. This may consist of scrambled egg and champagne or a bit of dry toast, according to your mutual requirements and the level of your foresight in such matters. There's something rather naughty – kind of like a midnight feast in reverse – about breakfast together in bed, and you would be unwise to overlook this sort of pleasure, even if taking breakfast is not normally a regular feature of your life.

A word of warning at this point. If you are not already aware of it, there is a peculiar phenomenon which afflicts toast while leaving other foodstuffs unaffected. Crumbs. It doesn't matter how careful you are, or how far from the bed it actually is. If you bring toast into a bedroom then the bed will swiftly fill up with crumbs. While this can be unpleasant the next night, when you attempt the act of sleeping upon a gravelled surface, it is even worse should you decide upon a repeat of the previous night's activity before getting dressed. Toast crumbs are remarkable things. In the same way that toast, when dropped, always falls butter side down, so also do toast crumbs find their way into the innermost recesses of the human body. If you got into a bed full of toast crumbs and lay perfectly still for as little as five minutes you would find the crumbs in your ears, between your toes, up your nose and also in a staggeringly wide variety of less-appealing locations.

Imagine, if you will, the truly horrifying prospects of getting into a bed full of toast crumbs and then performing a number of strenuous and intimate acts. Be careful with toast is all I've got to say.

After breakfast (or even before it) you may well feel like a little indulgence of a physical nature. This is quite in order, not to mention highly desirable. On the other hand you may well be of the type which cannot even speak in the morning, never mind anything else. Breakfast may help, it may not. If you do partake you may find that there are further opportunities available. Women, as we have previously observed, are fastidiously clean. It may well be that the next desirable item on her agenda is taking a bath. This you should offer, but not too pointedly, lest she gain the impression that you think she needs one. Even if you have missed out the early-morning physical jerks it may well be that the efforts of the night before now indicate that a bath would be desirable.

The very least you can now do is scrub her back and the best you can do is join her in. It is a fact that the average bath is designed to accommodate only one person at a time. Someone has got to have the taps. It is polite that this person should be you. Plugs are likewise a discomfort which a man may bear more readily than a woman. Remember this.

The next step, of course, will be getting dressed. This can be accomplished, by now, with a minimum of fuss. You may feel gentlemanly enough to offer her the run of your wardrobe. Many women like to wear their man's shirts. Take careful note here of the possessive pronoun. It implies a degree of belonging which you may well not wish to foster, and at the very best you may find that your favourite shirt is lost beyond recovery. Your future plans with regard to the lady must colour your decision in this matter, unless you can afford to give away shirts on an endless basis.

You must consider that the act of bathing with this delectable young lady may well lead you into further acts of a reprehensible but entirely desirable nature. This again is only right and proper and will, of course, depend upon whether or not you are both awake this early in the morning. It is a matter of personal preference, and you should not be influenced in this one way or another by anybody. Bet you can't help yourself, whatever you think right now. First time you lose the soap the matter will be decided . . .

If all this aquatic frivolity leaves you unmoved, or if time prevents you from indulging, you will still find there are other pleasures to be enjoyed. If it's her house she will doubtless rise first. If it's yours then you are urged to do the gentlemanly thing and accord her first crack at the bathroom. When she returns, do not spring into action yourself. Put off washing and shaving for a minute and stay in bed. Now is the moment at which you may watch her without fear, since all the previous night's intimacies should have removed the barrier of embarrassment.

Watching a woman getting dressed and ready to face the world is one of the greatest and most underrated pleasures life has to offer. Most men are so preoccupied with the business of getting a woman's clothes off that they totally ignore the moments at which she has to put them back on again.

But it is precisely now when you will be privileged to examine a rare and wonderful treat. Women go about their morning ritual entirely differently to men, and as they potter about in their underclothes, brushing their hair and applying their make-up, there is no moment in life at which they are more feminine, more vulnerable and more deserving of our admiration.

It is during this dressing ritual when their femininity asserts itself most strongly, and you should do your utmost to soak it all up; now is the moment, if you needed any confirmation, that you will be forcibly reminded of the female nature of the person you have spent the night with. Curled up in bed, you are able to luxuriate in the warmth of your recent experience and the moment at which, perhaps, you will feel emotionally closer to her than any other.

This is a truly wonderful delight, and should not be missed at any cost. You may admire her physique, marvel at the way her body moves, watch her in her most unguarded moments, all in a frank manner which would not have been possible the night before when you were both embarking upon your adventures and both, perhaps unconsciously, wearing a front, a public face, which will have evaporated as you slept.

In truth it is this moment for which you have striven so long, it is this sort of intimacy and closeness which has driven you together and to which all your efforts and scheming have been directed. Now is the time when you must heave pretence and sham right out of the window. It is this moment at which you are both most vulnerable. All your emotions will be on the surface and you will be without the protection of that veneer of cynicism with which so many people in our crowded society feel obliged to defend themselves.

Everything you do and say now will be of critical importance. *Omnes*, so they say, (or almost, anyway) *post coitus tristus est*, and never more so than the next morning. So think very carefully about what you say, lest you unwittingly indicate that the depth of your feeling and involvement is greater than it would have been were you only of sound mind.

Now, not last night, not tomorrow, but now, is the moment at which you must decide whether or not you are going to say goodbye or only *au revoir*. And it is the subtle little things which will make a difference; not only what you say but also what you don't say. Not only what you say but the way you say it; now only what you say but what you do. Now, before you open your mouth, you must decide what, if anything, you wish further from the lady who faces you across the room.

Saying Goodbye – or Maybe Just Au Revoir

Had we never lov'd sae kindly
Had we never lov'd sae blindly
Never met – or never parted
We had ne'er been broken-hearted
Robert Burns, *Ae Fond Kiss*

There used to be a time, way back in history, when being a professional messenger was a risky business. Aside from the hazards of footpads, felons and brigands there was always the possibility that some interested party or parties may have a compelling reason for preferring that the message did not reach its addressee. The simplest method of arranging this was to eliminate the middleman – the messenger. Even should none of this related or unrelated animosity transpire there was a further danger to be negotiated, namely the recipient of the missive. People in the habit of receiving messages on a regular basis tended to divide them arbitrarily into two kinds; good news and bad news. More often than not, history being as turbulent as it was, it would be the latter kind, although the message-bearers, being among the lower orders, were generally not appraised of the contents of the communication in advance. Which made delivery of same something of a heart-stopping moment, since bearers of bad tidings, having striven their utmost to do their duty and deliver the bulletin, were all too frequently put to a horrible and lingering death for their troubles.

Enlightenment seems to have crept into our modern world on this point at least, if not in many other areas of human barbarity, and few postmen or telephonists are put to death while engaged upon their legitimate employment. Nevertheless it is perhaps a sort of historical hangover which makes every one of us somewhat nervous when it comes to the dissemination of news which we have good reason to believe the recipient will look on as being wholly unpleasant. That, of course, plus a yellow streak a mile wide.

Consequently many of us will happily go to tortuous lengths in order to soften the impact of bad news, or better still arrange to have it imparted by some neutral person in our absence. Which may account for the success of the postal service, at least in part.

This abject dread is more often than not intensified when the bad news takes the form of the brush-off to some hapless females. Hell hath no fury, etc, and don't we all know it. Women have a pronounced tendency to stop being hapless and start being furious about this sort of thing, and their reaction is often one which makes the errant male wish he'd joined the Foreign Legion and gone off to fight the Dervishes instead of hanging about to face a veritable firestorm of abuse and assault.

This is generally a situation which comes about at the termination of a prolonged relationship rather than of two ships, having passed in the night, putting up their respective helms and sailing off to fresh adventures. It is nonetheless a moment which may be handled with tact and civility to greater advantage than with blunt truth.

Everybody has at one time or another laughed at the Noddy and Big Ears joke, in which Big Ears recommends to Noddy that he precipitately 'Fuck off'. Even were such an invitation to be prefaced with a polite 'please', it is not only the act of a bounder and a cad, it is also fraught with danger. Before you attempt a ploy of this nature ask yourself; how fast can you run?

Even thinking along this sort of line immediately establishes the fact that you will have no desire whatever to renew your acquaintance with the lady in question at some future opportune and otherwise unoccupied moment. This is the sort of decision you must take before you open your mouth and commit yourself to some irrevocable statement, whether it be to see or not to see at some other time and place.

If you're not worried about seeing her again then you clearly won't be worried about what you say to her or how you dismiss her. Although this means that you may use the blatant Noddy Formula with relative impunity as far as your future happiness is concerned, it doesn't mean that you will escape altogether unscathed, and you may find that you are summarily separated from several things you would rather have remained joined to, like your teeth. Let circumspection be your watchword, then, lest circumcision be forced upon you unrequested.

There are any number of ways in which you may communicate your lack of interest in the person before you and since you are disinterested it matters little which you choose. The only criterion is that you do not wish to be figuratively if not literally hung drawn and quartered when the bad news becomes public. Your personal wellbeing and comfort, your peace of mind, not to mention your safety, are therefore your prime concern.

In principle it would be far safer if you were able to withdraw from your priapic engagements saying nothing, aside from something like 'My God, is that the time, I really must dash', followed by a swift kiss on the cheek and an even swifter exit. This will absolve you from all future responsibility and is therefore the most desirable of any alternative. However it is quite likely that you will not be allowed to escape so easily, and that you will be forced to make some sort of arrangement for the future.

Your second line of defence must, therefore, be simply to obtain the lady's telephone number, scribble it on a petrol bill or a cigarette packet, tell her you'll call her soon and then don't. This will be sufficient to extricate you from most situations and should see you safely on your way. It might not, of course, if you are faced with a determined lady, or worse still one who has your phone number and may proceed to bombard you with phoned invitations to repeat your encounter.

This needn't be a bother, since you will quite easily be able to fend off such suggestions by protesting prior commitments. These may be as blunt as you wish, as truthful as you wish or as imaginary as you wish. Oscar Wilde once declined an invitation to a social gathering 'owing to a subsequent engagement'. George Bernard Shaw once received a printed invitation bearing the legend 'Mrs Wossname, At Home, Tuesday, 3.00pm–5pm' to which he replied in kind, his message reading simply 'Mr George Bernard Shaw likewise'.

Bluntness has a certain value, you see, but sadly for us the quaint habit of sending written invitations of this nature – giving you the opportunity to reply from a safe distance – has fallen into disuse, and far more often the telephone is the instrument of communication. You will discover at once that it is an act requiring far greater courage to be dismissive in person than in writing, which means that we must seek more acceptable ways of getting off the hook.

Being possessed of a genuinely full diary is a boon here, but it is no real bother to invent one should the need arise. Pretending a number of important and credible engagements is simple enough, and once the farce has gone on long enough all but the most persistent harpy will get the message.

It is a useful shortcut to such proceedings if you make your excuses as totally implausible as possible, thus getting the message over straight away and obviating the need for further embarrassing phone calls while you search your diary and imagination for reasons why you can't possibly go to the pub/cinema/disco/theatre/whatever.

The most direct of these is simply to decline her invitation since Thursday (or whenever it is) just happens to be the day when you have your second and, hopefully, final appointment at the special clinic . . . That usually clears the position up no end. You may of course find that the night she has in mind is the very night you are going to the hairdresser to have your artificial thatch re-woven, or you are obliged to take your 93-year-old granny to the pictures since she's been waiting ages and ages for you to escort her to a showing of *Emmannuelle Meets Rin-Tin-Tin at Emmerdale Farm*. Maybe you work nights as a male stripper or better still a drag artist, and no she can't come because they're private parties, if she gets your drift, know what I mean?

If you feel that this sort of thing is not within your own scope or perhaps not in your best interests (maybe she works with you, or knows you too well) then you will just have to resolve yourself to playing innumerable games of darts or pool until she goes away. Perhaps you could stop answering your phone, get someone to lie for you, ('No, I'm sorry, he's not here again. Yes, three weeks is kind of a long time to be on the potty, but he has been looking very pale just lately. All these late nights . . .'), or even institute a code – three rings, cut off and dial again, so that you can be sure it'll be someone you want to speak to on the other end.

If by bad luck you should slip up and get cornered, and find that you do have to take her out then your only chance is to make the evening as horrid as possible without being overtly rude. Talk about your experiences at the pox clinic, or the Magyar prostitute you met in Southampton the other evening. Treat it as a joke, her as your confidante, and don't forget to be surprised and hurt when she decides you're really an obnoxious toad and she never wants to see you again.

Of course you could just take her somewhere really appalling, like a genuine sawdust-and-fisticuffs pub where she's certain to be ogled and hounded by an endless succession of really awful geezers. You will wisely refrain from offering to champion her cause; you may even be surprised that she's not all that keen on the attention she's getting. After all, the other girls you bring here really find it quite exciting, and some of them have met some very nice friends here.

Then there's always strip clubs – which she's bound to hate – or porno movies (likewise, at least until she knows you better), or even the rugby club piss-up, during the entire course of which you will, naturally, ignore her completely until the the last possible moment. Then, from your comfortable position beneath some table or other, you will inform her as lucidly as you are able that unless she gets you home and you get down to business within the next few minutes you will almost definitely be sick, probably upon her person.

If all this fails, take her on a housebreaking expedition, or even cottaging. If, after one or several of these excursions she is still with you then think carefully about getting shot of her; you are in the presence of a rare woman, whose affections you would do well to cultivate. She sounds just like the sort of person you might need to navigate your creaking ship through the stormy sea of life and what-have-you. If she can also drink, cook, drive and tell one end of a three-pin plug from another then marry her. Or give me her phone number . . .

There is a possibility, which must not be overlooked, that it will be her who is doing all the not-so-fond farewelling. If this was what you had in mind in any case then this is all to the good. Do not fall into the trap of allowing your wounded masculine pride to intercede, leading you into attempts to persuade her to do otherwise, since if it works you will quickly find that not only are you faced with the burden of extracting yourself from a situation you didn't want in the first place, but she is now even more tenacious than she would otherwise have been. Women don't only have their mystique, you know – they also have pride, and frequently in far greater quantities than mere men would believe possible. If you had to fight to get her she'll fight even harder to keep you.

If her saying goodbye has no place in your plan of events then you will have to strive to change her mind or accept your fate and take it like a man. Should she reject your invitations for further rosy evenings together then there is little for you to do but regard her in the same light as you would any other long-term strategy, and you are referred to all previous advice on this subject. You will realise at once that this will be no time for pussyfooting about, and you must go straight into a full-out Blitzkrieg, beginning as soon as possible the same day if you can arrange it. The results of all this are entirely open to question. You will know when the time has come to give in gracefully.

And that is something you may wish to do on the spot, the minute she indicates that she wishes no further part of your life. You could become abusive and insulting, but it won't do anybody any good at all, and will only serve to show that she has got under your skin, which is not always a desirable state of affairs, since there are plenty of unscrupulous women who are more than ready to exploit such situations and take advantage of your sensitive nature. If you've got any such thing, that is . . .

Best thing is just take it like a man. Kill her.

Since the prospect of 30 years on a diet of beans and porridge is often less appealing than the alternatives you may simply choose to bite your tongue, grit your teeth (not while they're in the glass) and say nothing at all. At most you may choose to utilise the odd flash of humour, to show that you're a brave little soldier and don't mind at all. Rhett Butler has the monopoly on the clamp-jawed one-liner for this situatiuon; 'Quite simply, my dear, I don't give a damn'. Philistines who have not seen *Gone With the Wind* may care to note that the emphasis in this brief disclaimer is upon the word 'give', not 'damn' as you may have thought.

There are other exit lines available to you besides this one. You may console yourself with the thought that women are like buses: there'll be another one along in a minute, but you are advised not to give voice to this sentiment. Better to adopt the old showbiz precept and leave them laughing when you go. Something along the lines that when you were younger you used to hate girls who cried right afterwards, but now you hate the ones who laugh even more. You could even put up a token defence for yourself, and explain that you're not as good as you once were, but you're as good once as you ever were.

Perhaps a pouting statement to the effect that 'I never liked you anyway' will suffice, but with all lines of this nature it is the delivery which counts, lest she take you seriously instead of half-seriously or is just not certain if you meant it or not.

At times like this you should remember all your previous efforts at maintaining a stiff upper lip when getting the brush-off at the beginning of the evening. At least by now it will only be your lip that's stiff, and that's something to be grateful for at any rate.

It is a regrettable truism that women, while they may indeed be creatures of whimsy and may vacillate unbelievably in little things, like what dress to wear or which pair of shoes goes with which coat, are creatures of remarkable and stoic determination once they have actually made up their minds to do something of importance. You've only got to watch them driving. I know several ladies who drive a damn sight better than a great deal of men, but almost all of them fall prey to the fault of indecision. They'll linger behind a car, debating whether or not to overtake, for ages, missing several golden opportunities. Once they've made up their minds, though, they'll overtake at all costs, even if there's a lorry the size of a mobilised housing project coming at them from the opposite direction. Once they are decided upon a course of action there is little or nothing which they will allow to stand in their way, and are quite capable of demolishing a fully-equipped Panzer division single-handed if circumstances so demand.

If Madam has made up her mind that you are clearly unsuitable for any or all of the purposes she has in mind then she will write you out of her life on the spot, and there's precious little you can do about it. The odd roomful of priceless orchids may be enough to sway her if her decision was less than final, but anything more than that will remain as immutable as the Rock of rotten Gibraltar. The trick will be always to catch her at the stage before she has made this final decision. Of course all of this is as nothing when faced with the information that women will always reserve to themselves the right to change their own minds for the flimsiest of reasons, so you may still be in with a chance, at least for a while, even when all looks black.

Of course there is another, equally unpalatable possibility waiting in the wings for you. It is likely that your two aims may not entirely coincide and it will be her who has decided

to have you at all costs. We have already dealt with the moments at which you can successfully make your getaway before she's had a chance to decide – those persistent phone calls won't mean that she has definitely made up her mind that you are the one and only, but may only serve to indicate that she wishes to reserve judgement until later and is unwilling to let you depart until she is sure that she won't mind if you do just that.

If she has so adjudicated then the chances are that you won't be the first to know about it. In fact there's a better chance that you'll be the last to know, awareness only seeping into your sublimely indifferent consciousness long after the rest of the world has spotted you as a marked man.

Should your future plans not be of a coincidental nature you will begin to realise this, at whatever stage of the proceedings it occurs, when she begins to ask you questions like 'Do you love me?' Your possible answers to this starter for a damn sight more than 10 will fall into two categories. If yes then answer yes. If no, do not be so naive as to imagine that saying no will suffice or protect you from what will assume the mantle of a vicious and unprovoked attack. 'Why do you always start with the hard ones?' is better, having a humorous and deflective quality which may delay further discussion until you are sufficiently far removed from the front line as to guarantee your immediate safety if not your long-term immunity to further onslaught. 'Can I come back next week?' is another retort which may serve the same purpose.

At the same time you should be aware of the likelihood that she may well be at least as devious as you are striving to be, and will cloak her serious questions beneath a mantle of apparent levity. Beware, then, of queries like 'What do you think of it so far?' You will naturally turn this shaft aside with the traditional response – 'Rubbish'. Silly you to think that this was not what she was expecting or that she would be even remotely satisfied with such a crassly obvious reply. She will come straight back at you with something like 'No, I mean honestly?' It will then be too late for you to get out of it. Of an instant the previous lighthearted situation will have got out of hand faster than a bottle of meths disappearing down a wino's throat and you will be left facing a discussion fraught with incipient danger. You won't have seen it coming. Unprepared, you will be forced to bluster unconvincingly or own up to the truth. Either of these courses will lead you on to the rocks like an East Indiaman following a wrecker's lantern, with commensurate risk to life and limb. Worse things happen at sea, people always say. Pity it isn't always true, and an even greater pity that now is one of the times it isn't.

All of this represents the worse possible disaster concommitant upon your ignorance. As you sow, etc ... It is entirely conceivable that none of the aforementioned versions of Armageddon will transpire, and you will be faced with a lady you wouldn't mind seeing again, with a view to further transports of delight and unrestrained ferocity, and she will regard you in a roughly similar light. All that you need to do in this eventuality is ensure that she wants to see you again more than you want to see her. At very worst you should be attempting to put your desires on a more or less equable footing and thus maintain the *status* at least *quo*, if not more so.

If the morning after the night before is a weekend then all this will necessarily be simplified, because you will have at least part of the following day, if not all of it plus the following evening, in which to cement your relationship, while jointly embarking upon a voyage of mutual discovery in an attempt to ascertain who likes who and how much. This equable arrangement is without doubt to be preferred above all others but may not always be attainable.

If you must part almost immediately, or perhaps the following morning, then there will be the minimum of opportunity to construct anything of a semi-permanent nature from the skeleton of your night's adventures. Given small chance to flesh out the bones of your skinny corporate arrangements you will at once see the need to make some gestures of admiration and affection even though it may be neither possible nor desirable to profess undying love.

In this case your only course is to leave her feeling happy, contented, and that she is important to you in some way. In this task you will be much assisted if the desired impression at least approximates the truth. This should not be all that difficult, since all but the dimmest and personally objectionable of women are liable to inspire feelings of this type in all but the hardest of male hearts. This is entirely due to the fact that few women are completely devoid of that personality, that glimmer of compassion and that overwhelming sense of feminine beauty which makes it impossible for you to feel otherwise. Especially when they've got no clothes on and are vulnerable to your gaze and your thoughts.

If you have learnt anything by now it should be that all women are possessed of a common, yet individually unique value which is the very reason for our ardent pursuit of them. Once you have experienced it then it becomes impossible to forget and difficult to live without. Once you've got your hands on a real live example of the genre it becomes even harder (and in many cases rather stupid) to allow it to slip from your grasp.

This being so you will find it easy enough to say all the right things necessary to convince them of your genuine pleasure in their company and your earnest desire to repeat the experience at least several more times before you move on to other pastures. Nothing works as well here as does genuine belief in all of this. You will find it hard to conceal and even more arduous to fabricate. Most women will spot a sham in seconds, maybe less. Telling her you love her when you don't is a gambit unlikely to meet with a notable degree of success simply because she will almost certainly know you are fibbing. Thus, though it may be the oldest trick in the book, it's hardly worth bothering with. Romantic fiction is full of slimy toads who spirit otherwise sensible and practical girls away from the plain, but honest, son of the soil who truly loves her, blinding her avaricious eyes with tales of high living and mink coats, concealing his true and purely carnal intentions beneath a veil of insincere protestations of love. Everybody reading the book or watching the film can at once perceive that she is being horribly misled, but she remains sublimely indifferent to this massive truth until it finally falls on her from a great height. These heroines, if such be the correct terminology, are cast in the same mould as the idiot tarts in Hammer horror films, who enter the pitch-black coal cellar during a power cut even though they know their torch batteries have scant seconds to live and that some especially virulent form of unspeakable evil awaits them at the bottom of the stairs.

In short they are unbelievable, and do not exist in real life.

The question of total honesty, at moments like this, and at others, is worthy of lengthier and separate consideration, which we shall give it in the fullness of time. Meanwhile let it suffice to say that if your ambition is simply to attain further repetitive opportunities for a roll in the hay on subsequent occasions then affirming unswerving devotion is not the way to go about it. She will indubitably mark you down as a liar and a rogue, blowing you out of the window so fast that a smack from Friar Tuck will seem a blessing by comparison (Robin Hood had his moments, you know, despite all that dressing up in green stockings and frolicking in the woods with 30 assorted men of an avowedly merrie disposition).

Further guidance on treachery and deceit to follow, then. In the meantime you wish to ensure that you are given the benefit of a return fixture with the delectable lady currently putting on her face (and no cracks like – if she's got another why was she using that one all last night?) and making ready to leave both your domicile and your life, possibly forever unless you move fast.

We are agreed that nothing succeeds at moments like this better than honesty. So. You had a nice evening? You enjoy her company? You'd like to see her again? Then tell her so. If it's the truth you can't go wrong. She will have to believe you, since your frankness will be both disarming and convincing, and she cannot fail to be pleased and flattered by such a reaction. Let's face it, she has just admitted you to the most intimate and secret moments of her life. Any reaction other than happiness would be wounding to her, so she can't help being pleased that you took pleasure in all that has transpired. Nobody is more emotionally vulnerable than when they have just lowered all the barriers they normally erect to keep the world at large from gaining access to their private lives.

If you now tell her how much you've enjoyed being with her, and how much you'd like to do it again there is a more than passing chance that, because of your doubtless astounding personal charm and also the atmosphere with which you have managed to cocoon yourself over the preceding 12 hours or more, she will readily agree. It won't be necessary for you to imply any greater depth of meaning other than a desire to recreate the evening you have just shared in order for her to be suitably agreeable. It is reasonably important that you should accomplish this before you part company. Playing hard to get has its proper place in the scheme of things, but this isn't it. And you do need to secure her assent before she has gone to work and had her pleasant mood of euphoria blown asunder by the rip-roaring world of the early morning commuting hordes or the hurly-burly of business life. These sort of things are capable of defoliating a romantic idyll far more quickly than your habit of scratching your ear or picking your nose ever could, although it may be wise to remember this sort of thing and endeavour not to do them in public.

If, for any one of a variety of plausible reasons, you are unable to fix a date at which you will both be available to relive the experiences of last night you should not simply allow the matter to pass unresolved. You must at least agree in principle that such an event will be forthcoming, even if it must be postponed *sine die*. This is the very minimum level of commitment you must obtain before you can release her from your clutches.

Once you have parted it is not sufficient to allow events to run their natural course unaided by any human agency. You are the human agency in question, and you must make every effort to intervene if you want everything to progress according to your own perception of the desirable course of events.

Either you will have fixed up a time and place for your

next meeting or you won't. In any case this will not affect your next move, which will be the same in either eventuality. It is polite, to say the least, that you should contact the lady in reasonably short order. Preferably the same morning, maybe the next afternoon if you can't manage the morning, but at the very latest the following day.

This contact may take any one of a number of shapes. The most miniscule effort you can make will be to ring her, at home or at work, simply in order to reaffirm everything you said this morning before you parted company. This is a nice, polite and human thing to do, and whatever the final outcome of your liaison you will find no detriment and perhaps considerable benefit accrues from the observation of what are, after all, merely elementary courtesies such as you might award to a business colleague or acquaintance.

Since it is womankind we are dealing with here, and since we assume that your eventual intentions are to become far more intimately involved with her than you would ever dream of being with some bloke at work (and if last night doesn't prove that for definite then you have got something of a problem) it follows that while the minimum of effort will suffice it would be far more estimable if you could manage more than that. No need to go over the top, but a little more effort wouldn't hurt at all.

Such effort may take any form you wish; send her some flowers – this above all other moments in any relationship is the one at which flowers are not only acceptable and suitable but also unsurpassable – or a small gift. Small is the operative word here. Anything vastly expensive will at once give her the feeling that you are labouring under the misapprehension that her favours can be bought and paid for; even that you believe that they should be bought and paid for. The moment for expensive gifts has passed, and will not reappear for some little while. A fact for which, I have no doubt, both your bank manager and assorted credit card companies will be extremely grateful, if not actually effusive.

Don't fret about it; have you seen the price of flowers lately? A goodly crop of roses will set you back more of the green and folding than you could spend on drink in one night alone and expect to survive, so they're by no means cheap. And flowers, aside from being eminently apposite, also bespeak a far greater depth of interest than a phone call. If this is the impression you wish to give then carry on, but if it isn't you should reconsider before you send them and perhaps not bother at all, or possibly halve your expenditure, the size of the bouquet and, consequently, halve the effect it will have on her impressionable mind, causing her to abjure the erroneous beliefs she may have otherwise formed.

Halfway between flowers and a phone call comes the card; something light and airy, pleasant but not stifling, which will serve the useful purpose of bringing to her attention your thoughtfulness and the fact that you have gone to not inconsiderable trouble, although abstaining from vast expenditure. The only drawback to this remarkably valuable halfway house is that, the postal service being what it is, it cannot possibly arrive at her address until the following morning, and she may not even see it until the evening, almost two full days since your encounter. This is stretching it to a limit, since the speed of the follow-up is the critical factor. If the post does not suffice, or you can't get the whole thing together in plenty of time to guarantee next-day delivery then you may, if you can accommodate such action, take the card round to her house by hand. If you venture into this you must make absolutely certain that you do not come face to face with her while doing so. This will not only spoil the effect entirely, it may even do great harm to your cause. If she is otherwise engaged you will embarrass her considerably; enough to stop her seeing you again even though she would have been quite happy to do so had you not showed up when you did. Even if she isn't occupied, but catches you in the act of delivery she will almost certainly feel obliged to invite you in for coffee at the very least. While this may fit in with your plans admirably enough it might throw hers into confusion. If she'd wanted to see you tonight she would have arranged to do so (since you must have already asked . . .); the fact that she wasn't expecting you means that, for any one of a multitude of good reasons, she didn't want your company tonight. You are now, in her eyes, forcing yourself upon her. While determination and persistence are admirable qualities which have often won over an indecisive heart the timing is presently all wrong. You do not belong where you have not been invited, at least not yet. If she thinks that you could well turn into the clinging grapevine type you could well find that you've been given your discharge papers before you'd even accepted your commission.

If you can't send her something in the post in sufficient time, you don't want to send her flowers, but you'd still like to make a gesture slightly more flamboyant in nature than ringing her up, send her a telemessage. Since these little swines cost an absolute fortune you would be well advised to keep wordage to an absolute minimum. In any case telemessages are impersonal articles, quite without the charm and pleasing aspect of a card or a message accompanying a few flowers, and are clearly not the place for sentimental verbiage. It would, since telegrams are of necessity read by a wide variety of people before they arrive at their destination, be singularly inappropriate to include heated references to the wonderful night you have just spent together. Far better to confine yourself to simple statements in the 'Thanks for everything, looking forward to Tuesday' vein. Not that you should need to be told this sort of thing by now.

In fact there are few things left which you do need to be told, as most things will become clearer as you put them into practice on a repetitive basis. And although we haven't been setting any tests, you have been practising, have you not? Well enough.

There only remain to us a few disparate elements to deal with which do not rightfully belong elsewhere and have consequently been left to the very end. One such, you will recall, is treachery, which must only be used as a last resort in any eventuality. We will proceed at once to the examination of the deceit which the human male is capable of. Also the human female, which is far less appealing . . .

Honesty – Before and After

Women and elephants never forget an injury
Hector Hugh Munro, *Reginald on Besetting Sins*

Always provided that you've been paying attention you can't have failed to notice that we've successfully managed to divide most situations into a simple question of dual choice. Either/or decisions are always the easiest, and a little bit of thought should suffice to reduce most dilemmas to this sort of manageable level. To what the more pompous among us might be tempted to call an essential dichotomy, were they only so well-read.

There is always one problem which you will be bound to encounter sooner or later (sooner, if you've got my luck) and that is whether or not you need to be, or are obliged to be, honest with the ladies you meet. This is a decision which nobody can actually make on your behalf, although there are a number of people who may feel it incumbent upon themselves to offer you advice. Not all of this will always be that well-meant, but you should find it relatively easy to pick out the obvious ill-temper. Suggestions that you go play on the nearest motorway, for example, won't need an awful lot of thought. The subtle stuff you'll have more problems with, I'm afraid, and the best thing is to ignore most of it, if not all. Aside, that is, from what I'm about to tell you. You can trust me . . .

Adolf Hitler may have been a great number of diverse things, not many of which concern us here, but among his accomplishments he could count the fact that he was no mean psychologist, nor yet a bad liar. The rule he worked to in this last matter was derived directly from his ability in the first. What he said was that if you are going to tell porkies you are best advised to tell whoppers. Let's face it, once you've started it doesn't make a lot of difference what level of duplicity you go in for. The sin is one of commission and once committed may as well be utilised to the full. More importantly most people will more readily believe a big lie than they will a small one, for reasons which escape me entirely. This practical information is in no way intended to influence your conscience in any way; your truthfulness or otherwise is entirely your concern. There will doubtless come, however, at least one and probably several moments at which it will seem advisable that the truth, if not actually twisted or ignored altogether, should at least remain discreetly hidden. The art of not divulging any information whatsoever, especially when to do so would be injurious to the cause, is a delicate one filled with subtle nuances and pastel shades of grey rather than distinctive blacks and whites. It won't serve many useful purposes at the initial moment when you meet a new lady, although it could well come in dead handy later on. To begin with you will find that fibbing will be more valuable than concealing unpalatable truth through silence. If she asks you what your job is and you choose not to reveal that your gainful occupation is, say, unbunging blocked drains, remaining silent won't solve anything. On the other hand providing the information that your job is a complex one to do with the routing of inland waterways will work wonders, and it isn't entirely untrue.

Once again the factor which will probably influence your veracity to the greatest extent will be your future intentions. If you never want to see the girl again then you may come out with as many whoppers as you find amuse you, as long as they do not strain her credulity beyond breaking point.

However there is no harm, especially when effecting an introduction of yourself to ravishingly attractive women, in telling the largest fibs you can conjure up. You know, about your Dad being an eccentric billionaire, or how you're a brain surgeon on a year's sabbatical, or a Russian defector living under an assumed identity. Very often the application of ruses like this may enable you to win a certain amount of success with a woman which would beyond all doubt have eluded you had you announced that, aside from pimples and a jacked-up Cortina, all you had to your name was a job as an insurance clerk and a town house in Basildon.

Not that she will believe any of the palpable rubbish you've just fed her. My word no. But then, it isn't important that she should. In many instances it will be better if she doesn't. Women tend to like men with a sense of humour, and if you can make her laugh then you'll be doing well. In order for this happy state to come about it is important that you do not give the impression that you expect her to believe the lines you've been shooting, but simply allow the pair of you to extract the maximum entertainment value from them.

The clear danger here is that you may take it all too seriously yourself, and instead of laughing with you she'll be laughing at you. You may think that you're getting on a treat, and that she really believes all that rot about you being Mick Jagger's bodyguard. Don't kid yourself. She'll be taking the juice like crazy, and after she's had as many laughs as she thinks are available she'll vanish so fast you'll think the Invisible Man was an eyesore.

Keep your tongue well and truly planted in your cheek at all times, then. This will serve you well in two directions. First she'll enjoy your humour, and second, when it all becomes so transparent that even a blind chimpanzee could see through it all you'll be able to pass it all off as a pleasant joke. This will save you from appearing to be something of a prize buffoon at the precise moment when you can least afford such upsets.

And, as you well know yourself, clairvoyance is not something you can truthfully catalogue among your many talents (although a passing ability to read palms, or pretend that you can, may well help you to meet still more women).

Thus you will never know when some young thing you at first thought of as a passing fancy may turn into a longer-term subject of your affections. This will doubtless mean that all your previous fibs will catch up with you and you will be found out. One-night-fancies will not matter, but if, after you have decided to propagate a deeper and more meaningful relationship she suddenly discovers that you tell more lies than Arthur Daly and bumps you out, the personal distress caused could well prove unacceptable.

If you have been telling fibs and you decide to prolong your acquaintance it will be in your best interests to unburden yourself of the truth as soon as you can manage it. Make a joke of it, by all means, but do make sure you tell her yourself, because if she works it out for herself, or worse still finds it all out from a third party then your life won't be worth living.

The majority of the time you will discover that coming clean is not as difficult as you may have surmised. Indeed, owning up to a lot of old rubbish and saying frankly that you only made it up to meet her or impress her, because you really wanted to go out with her but were afraid she wouldn't look twice at you if you told the truth, can be a disarming and even enchanting compliment. It might even win you more favour in her eyes than you previously enjoyed when you were some kind of filthy rich megastar.

Another delightful facet of human nature comes to light here. People who confess to fibs, and in the process of so doing diminish themselves in the eyes of their confessor, will often win a great deal of sympathy. This is a valuable emotion worthy of much cultivation. It is also something you may care to bear in mind when you decide to open negotiations on a strictly truthful basis. Tell lies which make you out to be a bit of a berk, or a bit less clever than the person you're fibbing to and they're almost certain to believe you. No one, they will reason, makes up untruths which ridicule themselves.

So tell whoppers if you're telling them at all, and try to run yourself down a little – not too much – while doing so.

The moments for little white lies – or bloody great big

ones – is right at the beginning of the evening, or maybe later on during its initial stages. This is all well and good, and part of the innumerable courtship rituals which women expect from men and men expect from women at such moments. However there comes a time in every relationship when both parties are expected to embark upon a course of reasonable, if not total, honesty. Some quirk of human nature dictates that this moment will be synonymous with the removal of your clothing. For some unknown reason people do not expect you to lie to them once they are naked, although there seems no definable information as to why this should be so. But it is.

If you lie your head off when picking up a young girl the world at large (and she in little) will regard you as nothing more than a humorous rogue with an advanced sense of fun. Once you have jointly entered into the world of fornication the story becomes entirely different, and you will find that only full-blown heels and bastards lie to their bedmates, and deceptions even of a trivial nature will earn you more active dislike than ever before. It's the same principle as we apply to politicians. Everybody expects them to fib during a campaign, but God help them if they do it once they get into office.

Particularly unsporting is misleading the lady as to your marital status. While it is quite in order – and often very useful – to say you are married when you aren't, simply in order to rid yourself of an unwanted encumbrance, to do the reverse is to open a whole new can of worms. You simply cannot tell a lady you're not married when you are and hope to get away with it.

Aside from any other considerations she will notice lots of little things which tend to give you away. She will also soon work out the reasons behind the fact that you are only available to her on odd occasions at very short notice. Furthermore she will soon get wise to the fact that she never meets your friends or gets to visit your house.

Even if you think she deserves nothing better from you than trickery and treachery, even if the whole world knows that she didn't get where she is today by taking in washing, nobody will forgive you for leading her up this particular garden path. She's going to twig anyway, as we've said, so there's no use in prolonging this sort of thing unless you thought that the first night was a one-off and have now had cause to revise your opinion.

Once again you must own up at once, yourself, and in person. However unpalatable the truth may be she will take it better from you than from another. And it's no use giving her all that old blarney about your wife not understanding you. Madam you are talking to will know only too well that your wife almost certainly does understand you and very clearly indeed, which is how you got into all this bother in the first place.

The confession of previous misdemeanours is far harder and far more distressing if it follows intimacy than if it precedes it – whatever the felony may have been. Confession need not necessarily preclude the hoped-for intimacy taking place, either; a lot of people, including women, get a certain thrill out of doing something naughty, and there's no reason why that something shouldn't be you.

Also you will find two-timing, even if the unfortunate cuckold isn't actually your spouse, can be a great strain. You spend interminable evenings wondering if you've been spotted, wondering if you're staying out too late and wondering whether you can get out of spending the night with this one without causing her too much grief (you can't – she'll know when something's amiss without you ever having to open your mouth). You suffer horrid and excruciating pangs of conscience about the little lady you've left moping at home, not to mention the kids. Make no mistake, there are few people in this world who are well-enough equipped to carry off a prolonged programme of duplicity without getting caught and almost none who can manage it without suffering tortures of conscience.

Sooner or later, whether you're married or not, whether you feel you owe the ladies in your life any debt of honesty or not, you are going to forget your cover story, forget where you were last night, fail to recognise that voice on the phone in time to prevent yourself from making a fatal

blunder, or just crack up under the strain and be carried to the ambulance foaming at the mouth and biting the sleeve of your jacket.

And your friends; they may be happy to cover for you at first, they may even think it's something of a joke, but sooner or later they're going to forget and drop you in it or, even more unpleasant, just get fed up with the whole sordid business and abandon you to the wolves.

Even the long arm of coincidence can reach out and grab you by the curlies. You may not necessarily feel that the Gods punish all transgressors in the end, but sometimes it can be hard to avoid the feeling that someone up there has taken a dislike to your activities and decided to bring them to a precipitate and unpleasant halt.

I was two-timing once. Oh, all right, more than once. These particular two were not, shall we say, inter-conscious. One evening, stuck in the sort of jam which we have just been speculating about, it became desirable (or rather imperative) that both received a visit. This they duly were given, both visits being of an understandably brief duration. Congratulating himself on his all-round smartness, yours truly retired to bed. Next morning, on Victoria Station, in a rush-hour crowd exceeding 200,000 souls, these two ladies met and, quite by chance, exchanged experiences. They retired together for coffee and there exchanged a few more. The net result of all this being that one of us (no prizes for guessing) was done up like a kipper by both of them. Now tell me you don't believe in divine intervention.

If you propose to indulge in excesses of the flesh on an indiscriminate basis then you are advised to ensure that a similar fate does not befall you. The only way in which this can be guaranteed is via a passing amount of truthfulness. If you're not going to see one lady tonight because you already have an appointment with another then don't tell her you're playing pool with the boys. You don't actually have to tell her what you are doing, but don't fabricate a story which may easily be shot down in flames.

The best situation of all is to cultivate the friendship of modern-minded girls who don't give a stuff what you get up to as long as you show up when you say you are going to and behave towards them as they would wish you to. This kind of Nirvana is, sadly, exceptionally rare. Whatever the Sunday supplements may have you believe, liberation is a concept which so far has not got past the planning committee in the female mind, still less attained widespread maturity and acceptance.

Infidelity, if that is what it should correctly be termed, is by no means the only form of dishonesty open to practitioners of the big lie. There are many others, most of which we have already encountered at one stage or another. One which we have so far skirted around in a discreet and genteel manner is perhaps even more offensive than all the others put together.

Doubtless you will recall that we dealt very early on with the question of personal hygiene. Your ears, let it now be clearly understood, are by no means the only portions of your body capable of gathering foreign matter and retaining it in the form of dirt. There are other places which are equally susceptible to this sort of thing if not more so. You won't need to be told about this I'm sure. You may need a gentle reminder, though, to the effect that washing assiduously with soap and water will not always eradicate alien substances. These may often take the form of particles or organisms too small to be recognised by the human eye, in which case they are a mild irritant at least, maybe worse. If they are worse they tend to go under the generic heading applied to all sexually-transmitted diseases of an unsocial nature; VD.

This is something you will catch in the same way as you get a cold; from someone else. It is, generally speaking, invisible at first, having no discernible symptoms like copious and frequent sneezing which may caution you to stay clear of persons suffering from the common cold.

The advent of the pill has meant that the incidence of all types of VD (and there are a great many more varieties than you may have thought) has increased dramatically. Over a long period of promiscuity there is a fair chance that you will encounter it sooner or later. Sexually transmitted diseases no longer carry the stigma that they used to. Anybody, provided they indulge, can catch one and quite some of the nicest people have suffered at one time or another. In the majority of cases the complaint is reasonably harmless, although irritating, provided it is treated promptly.

If it happens to you the best thing you can do is shut up and take your pills (but no alcohol) for three weeks or however long a cure takes, before rejoining the world at large. Whatever you do there is no question that you would knowingly pass on an illness, whatever it may be, so you will most certainly adopt a lifestyle of abstinence and restraint. Right?

The unpleasant news is that you may have already passed the disease on before you became aware that you were a sufferer, in which case you have no alternative but to backtrack and warn all those likely to be affected. This is not a subject which should be open to any debate, and there is no room for any beliefs other than those which indicate that in this, if in no other matters, honesty is your only option.

Remember; it's no shame. The nicest people can get it. After all, you caught it somewhere, didn't you? Yes. Anyone can have it. What about that nice fresh-faced blonde nymphet lying next to you right this minute? Even her, pal, even her.

So many people are lonely in our crowded cities these days, and so many of them mistake the act of sexual congress for love, that it is no wonder there's so much of it about. You've only got to look at the personal columns of newspapers and magazines to know that. And while we're on the subject, that's something we haven't thought about up until now.

It is not for me to suggest that you should advertise in newspapers as a way of meeting girls, although for a great number of people who truly are desperately shy there is no doubt that it is not only their last hope, but that it can also be successful. Some people find this easier because the impersonal advert requires a definite response. It reverses the normal situation and means that someone has to come to them rather than the other way around. They also know that anyone answering the ad is likely to be as shy and desperate as they themselves, as well as sympathetic to the advertiser's needs. This absolves them of most of the responsibilities normally attendant upon meeting persons of the opposite sex, including most of the worries. It works in exactly the same way for the respondent as well, and in this fashion may be deemed to be entirely satisfactory as a method of forming friendships, relationships and even for simply getting laid.

Though you may not feel the need to advertise in these columns yourself, you may decide that they offer a rich stamping-ground for anyone patient enough to write the letters and wait for the answers. You could be right. Be advised of two things. First, a great number of such ads are little better than a come-on, either designed to take your money in some way and at some future date, or for the poor perverted sod who placed the ad to get his rocks off at your expense. Note, if you will, that the great preponderance of these sort of pleas are placed by men, which would be a good enough reason for suspecting all the ones purporting to be from women even without the crusading efforts of the tabloid press.

This doesn't mean that none of them are genuine, but there are good grounds for retaining a small amount of caution in all such cases. Be fair, placing an ad in the personal column of a newspaper doesn't necessarily make you a bad person, but a great number of such advertisers were more than likely bad people before they started.

As a matter of moral conscience it may appear to you that preying on the genuine advertisers, who are almost certainly, if only by virtue of their natural timidity, more vulnerable than average, is something of a low act. Be sure, therefore, of your own motives, also those of others you may encounter through this medium.

There is another option open to you in this field, and it is that of computer dating. There are several organisations offering this service, and although they do make a charge they also tend to come up with the goods fairly often. In this matter you will find that it will definitely pay you to be scrupulously honest, otherwise you'll be wasting your time and your money. If you describe yourself as resembling Robert Redford when you don't look as much like him as you do Ernest Borgnine then you will be immediately found out. In any case most of these services will require you to supply a photograph of yourself in order to confirm that you're not a bigger fibber than all of the Borgia Popes put together. And if you wish to meet a blonde nymphomaniac with a view to committing unnatural acts as frequently as possible then it will behove you to say so, otherwise you'll keep getting introduced to a succession of Sunday-school teachers with no interest whatever in the trunk of sexual appliances you keep under your bed. This, too, is clearly a great waste of time, mostly yours.

Other people who are prone to, shall we say, misunderstand your lighthearted assertions of deep emotion immediately prior to being admitted to your bedchamber are ladies of a foreign disposition. Accents, strange parentage and different backgrounds can be most alluring, and it is quite understandable that you should be susceptible to this sort of thing. However, beware of allowing your mouth to operate at a speed which is very much greater than your brain's pedestrian activity, since you may well find that one of them will misconstrue an invitation to share your bed as being of a permanent rather than a temporary nature.

This is not something which you may safely ignore should you meet the lady on her home territory while you are on holiday or away on business, and you must beware of the doorstep jobs. You wouldn't be the first homing Briton to answer his door two weeks later to find a suitcase-laden continental waif expecting to move in and share a life of bliss forthwith.

No doubt about it, there are times when honesty is the best policy, and even more times when a gilded but forked tongue has led its owner into deep waters. There's no telling when it could be your turn, and you should remember what we said at the very beginning; when you're dealing with a force of nature as complex as woman, you're on your own. Which is probably just what you wanted all along.